Golf for Beginners

Barney Beard
1st Edition

Other Books by Barney Beard

Chapter Books

The Bow Window

The Amazing Adventure of Carter and the Pie Rats
New England Book Festival-Award Winner

The Incredible Adventure of the Eight Cousins
FAPA Silver Medal Winner

The Book Visitors

The Strolin' Dolan

The Horrible Word Hole

The Great Alphabet Adventure

Summer of '19

Their New, Big, Old House

Shut Up and Dance

The Ordinary Man and the Book Dragon

Luke and Carter: Their Summer Adventure

Melody and Connor: Christmas with Grammy

Melody and Connor: Their Visit with Grammy

Oliver and Quinn Travel in Space

Luke and Carter's Winter Adventure

Books for Early Reading

Five Little Monkeys

Conner Can Read

Our Favorite Nursery Rhymes

Luke's Great Adventure Begins

Carter Finds His Imagination

Quinn's Great Adventure

Oliver Learns to Read

More Books by Barney

The Old Man and the Book

Where We keep our Indians
Historical Novel

The Ordinary Man: A Poem
New England Book Festival Winner-First Place

Golf for Beginners
Double Award Winner-FAPA Silver & eLit Bronze

Letters to My Grandchildren

My Collected Poems

The Adventures of Bouncy

Letters to My Grandchildren: Volume II

The Official Rules of Canasta

Golf for Beginners: Left Hand Version

How to Write: A Primer
New England Book Festival Winner-First Place

Writer's Journal
Award Winner-eLit Bronze

A White Killing Frost
New England Book Festival Honorable Mention
Historical novel woven around the Cherokee Nation's
deportation from northwest Georgia. 1820-1838. 744 pages.

Table of Contents

Golf for Beginners

Barney Beard

1st Edition

ISBN 978-1-957179-01-8

Contact:
barneybeardgolf@yahoo.com

Go to my golf blog for more golf articles
Barneybeardgolf.wordpress.com

Author's Preface

I hope you find this little book useful. I certainly enjoyed writing it. It's a pleasure to share with you what I've spent many years learning from my students. Without a doubt, I've learned a great deal more from my students than they learned from me. I owe each one a huge debt of gratitude.

If you're going to be in central Florida, give me a shout and schedule that first complimentary lesson. Your first thirty-minute, private golf lesson with me is free and there's no obligation.

I wish you all the best and wish for you and yours many happy, carefree days on the golf course.

Play Often, Have Fun, Respect the Game,

Barney Beard

Phone: 352-638-4180
Email: barneybeardgolf@yahoo.com
Website: barneybeardgolf.com
Blog: barneybeardgolf.wordpress.com

This book is dedicated to:

Alice Helene
and
Samuel Emerson Beard

This book is dedicated to my constant parents who raised me to be a responsible adult and taught me to love many things, one of which is the game of golf. There isn't a child in the world who had a more loving childhood than I experienced in their home.

If you put the hay down where the calves can get it…
…the cows can get it too.

Purpose of this Book

This book is written for beginners. I shall do my best to share the things I've learned over a lifetime to help you get on the right track as you develop into the best golfer you can be.

However, not only will this book be good for beginners, but I think it would also be useful to any experienced golfer who wants to lower their handicap.

When I was a teenager I often did part-time work for Mr. Dave Shaver on his dairy farm. Mr. Shaver's place backed onto my Dad's property in Walker County, Georgia, about twenty miles south of Chattanooga, Tennessee on Highway 95. Every summer I would help Mr. Shaver haul hay. It was a great way to make extra money for any teenager who didn't mind a little hard work—well, a lot of hard work, actually.

What does hauling hay for Mr. Shaver have to do with teaching golf?

That's a good question. I'll tell you the answer. Mr. Shaver needed a lot of hay to feed his big Holstein milk cows and their little calves during the cold winter months when the lush green grass of summer went dormant. He had a large dairy herd. I guess we drank a lot of milk.

Mr. Shaver said the principle of feeding his dairy herd was simple. This is what he taught me:

He said, "Barney, if you'll put the hay down where the calves can get it, the cows can get it, too.

Make it simple and everyone can learn.

1

For the Love of the Game

Golf is played in nature's broad arena on acres and acres of beautifully manicured landscape in a serene environment that suits the human soul.

When I play golf I'm privileged to enjoy some of the most charming greenscapes in the world. Flowers, shrubs, lawns, trees, forests, streams, rivers, lakes, birds and wildlife greet me on every side. When I'm on the golf course, I'm royalty.

I play a game of infinite possibility while walking, talking, laughing and enjoying the camaraderie of my playing companions. What a wonderful sport played through open meadows and down broad avenues of stately trees.

No two golf courses are alike, no two holes are alike and no two days are the same. Golf brings to me a multifaceted joy that transports me to a place of unrivaled peace. On the golf course distractions melt away. It is said, and I believe it to be true, that it is impossible to bring one's worries to the golf course. No wonder so many love the game.

Several years ago I was on the practice tee. I heard a noisy foursome putting out on the adjacent 8th green. I couldn't see them because of dense shrubbery, but I heard them. As someone's putt rolled towards the hole, the four unseen players became louder and louder. Their excitement was contagious. Even an old veteran like me couldn't prevent a sympathetic grin as I imagined someone's long putt curving down the hill and rolling into the middle of the hole. I love this game.

Golf is Addictive

When I was a little boy my father loved to fish and hunt. He was a hundred percent country and taught me to love the outdoors. I remember spending long lazy days at the lake in a small boat or fishing from the bank with my father and mother. I remember swimming. I remember eating beside the water. There is nothing to compare with eating fish just out of the skillet cooked on an open fire close beside the water's edge—a fish you caught yourself only 30 minutes ago.

My dad never played any kind of sports. I cannot remember my father watching any sporting event on television except golf. He never liked baseball or football and thoroughly despised basketball.

When I became enamored with golf in primary school, I wanted golf clubs for Christmas. My mother told the story of how she asked my father if it would be ok to buy me a beginner set of golf clubs as a Christmas present. My father didn't like the idea because he thought golf the dumbest of games—even more stupid than basketball.

"There really couldn't be a point to golf, could there?" he would say. "How could hitting a little white ball repeatedly with a crooked stick in a cow pasture be fun?"

My dad said to my mother when she asked him about buying me golf clubs for Christmas, "If you buy the boy golf clubs, I will never play golf with him—never in a hundred years."

When she told this story, she would smile as she glanced over at my Daddy. My father has a strong history of sticking by his word so my mother and I figured I was pretty much on my own with golf, but then my Mom knew my Dad and perhaps she anticipated something in our future my father didn't quite foresee.

I got my golf clubs for Christmas. I can close my eyes fifty years later and see every detail of my precious gift. It was the most beautiful beginner set of golf clubs Sears & Roebuck ever sold. The set had a little black imitation leather bag with a 3, 5, 7 and 9 iron. Along with the irons there was a putter and a magnificent burgundy finished wooden driver and matching three wood. Yes, they were made of real wood in those days. I still call them woods. I don't care what Johnny Miller says, I have a wood even though it's hollow and made entirely of metal.

What more could a child possibly want? The only gift that rivaled my golf clubs was my Daisy BB gun. I didn't know it at the time but the BB gun was soon doomed to neglect.

I was in primary school in Rock Spring, Georgia that Christmas. I was much too young to drive myself to the golf course in Lafayette, the county seat of Walker County. My father and mother took turns ferrying me to the golf course in our new white '63 Plymouth Fury. If you or anyone you know ever owned a '63 Plymouth Fury you'll never forget the look of the front end of that car, but I didn't care. Kids don't care about those things, do they? My mom and dad must have got a great deal.

Sometimes Daddy would wait at the veranda of the clubhouse for me to finish my round. He's a patient man. One day my Dad was bored waiting for me to finish my round and Nathan, the golf pro, was also bored. I wish I had a video of that first meeting.

From that day if Nathan saw my Daddy waiting for me on the long veranda of the clubhouse on the top of the hill under the tall southern pines, a vista that overlooked the entire golf course, Nathan would stop what he was doing and chat with Daddy.

4

It wasn't long before Daddy and Nathan were friends and then soon after, close friends. Nathan was a full-blooded, witty country boy like my father. Nathan was well traveled. He was a people person with a remarkable knack for story-telling. Years later Daddy would say he knew Nathan wasn't a liar because Nathan always repeated his stories exactly the same way every time.

Nathan had been on the pro tour for a few years when he was young and played with men like Byron Nelson, Henry Picard, Horton Smith and Jimmy Demaret. He had the most interesting tales to tell about the greats from the 30's and 40's and 50's. I wish I had written those stories down. You would have loved them.

I was a little boy in those days. I didn't care if my face was dirty, if my hair was sticking straight up or if I had holes in the knees of my jeans. I could never remember to bring my jacket home from school in the warm spring afternoons. When I was a boy listening to Nathan, it never occurred to me to write down his stories. It never occurred to me that one day I would want to remember every word of every story Nathan ever told.

Somewhere early in their friendship, Nathan persuaded my father to have a timid whack at a golf ball. My dad took his experimental swing at a golf ball and the rest is history. That's how my father took up cow pasture pool.

I'm not sure it was love at first whack, but it wasn't long before my dad bought an old, ugly, worn-out set of First Flight irons from some guy who worked in the pipe shop at Dupont in Chattanooga. I remember those irons. They were beat up and worn, the metal shafts speckled with rust, Daddy stripped the threads out of the nylon grips to make them easier to hold in hot weather. They were ugly and cheap. Daddy grew up during the depression and he was thrifty. He used those raggedy old clubs for years.

It was only a matter of weeks before we began playing golf every Saturday and Sunday till I left home for college. There isn't a boy in the United States who has better memories of his father, his mother and golf than I.

Gowf Came from Scotland

No one really knows for sure how far back in history people played gowf. Many historians believe some form of gowf was played in the 1300's. It's suspected that gowf began on the rabbit runs lining the dryer Eastern sea shore of Scotland when young, competitive, bored Scotsmen developed a game by hitting round stones down the shoreline into distant rabbit burrows.

It's known in 1457 the pastime was banned in the English military by King James II because his archers were spending more time trying to get a little ball into a rabbit hole than an arrow into a target. But, as you can guess, the ban on gowf, like any ill-thought-out prohibition, was doomed. In 1502 the fruitless law prohibiting the enjoyment of the links by the military was lifted officially by the politicians in the Treaty of Glasgow.

At some point an industrious young Scotsman decided a crude rabbit burrow or a hand dug hole wasn't sufficient for their high purposes, so they borrowed, probably late at night and without permission, a drain pipe from a nearby dwelling, cut it in short lengths and replaced the earthen rabbit burrows with their neat, purloined metal drain pipe. Into each hole they placed a standard with a flag. Today, the same as in the 16th century, we have a four and quarter inch drainpipe size hole. Don't we wish that the industrious Scottish lads who borrowed the drain pipe had decided to use the larger sewer pipe instead.

The first recorded international gowf match was played in 1682. The Scots dominated competitive gowf for a century or two. It wouldn't be until the beginning of the 20th century before Harry Vardon, the magnificent English golfer, would permanently end the Scots' world dominance. Today on the PGA Tour, the golfer with the best scoring average of the year is awarded the Vardon Trophy in honor of Harry Vardon.

The Saint Andrews Golf Club has documented records back to its founding in 1754. The R&A, as it is called today, is partners with the USGA governing golf and the rules of golf.

In the 1800's, golf spread from Scotland in an enthusiastic world pandemic. In the early days, golf, like tennis, was pretty much the pastime of the privileged. It wouldn't be until well into the 20th century before the lower-class golf professionals would even be allowed into the elite clubhouse to change their shoes during a competition.

Gowf was spreading like wildfire in the United States. In 1913 a young Massachusetts man, Francis Ouimet, defeated two Englishmen, Harry Vardon and Ted Ray, in a Monday playoff for the United States Open Championship. Against all odds the young Mr. Ouimet won the tournament. After Mr. Ouimet's win, the young man was carried off the course on the shoulders of several thousand fanatical fans of the new sport. To this day Francis Ouimet is the only man to have ever been carried off a golf course in the United States after a win.

With Mr. Francis Ouimet's unexpected and popular win, gowf exploded into the sport we know today. Do yourself a favor and read the book and see the movie, *The Greatest Game Ever Played.*

Better yet, let's you and I play gowf today.

Learning
the
Game of Golf

That Strange Game
It's like backing a trailer

One day a nice lady stopped me in the middle of her golf lesson. With hands on her hips, she gave me a sour look and said, "You've got me doing this backwards. I don't get it. You want me to swing down at the golf ball to make it go up. Hitting a golf ball is like backing a trailer. Everything in golf is the opposite of what it should be."

She wasn't angry. She was simply expressing her confusion. I was trying to teach her to swing down at the golf ball in order to make it fly. Her instinct was to swing up. If she tried to swing up at a golf ball lying on the ground, she would only manage to hit the top of the golf ball and the result would be ugly. You see her problem, don't you?

We went on to have a good lesson, but I'll never forget the dramatic way she communicated her frustration.

The lady was right. Making a golf ball do what you want is like backing a trailer while looking in your rear-view mirror.

Everything is backwards about golf, isn't it?

If you want the ball to fly, you swing down on it.

If you want it to go to the right, you line up to the left.

If you want it to go to the left, you line up to the right.

If you swing with all your might, the ball won't go very far.

If you swing effortlessly, the ball goes great distances.

Tense your muscles and the ball goes into someone's yard.

Swing as if you didn't care and the ball goes straight.

The harder you try, the worse your score.

I remember one golf match when I was on the Lafayette High School golf team last century. That sounds like a very long time ago, doesn't it? Well, I remember this day clearly.

From the first hole I played poorly. I was terrible. We played match play and after about six or seven holes I was well behind my opponent. I think I lost every hole. I was spraying the ball all over the golf course. When I swung at my golf ball it felt like I was hitting a brick with a broken two-by-four.

Well, like only a petulant teenage boy can do, I decided the match was out of reach and I had no chance of winning. I gave up. I decided I would no longer attempt to play well. I was disgusted. When it came my turn to play, I walked up to the ball and swung without thinking. I didn't care where the ball went.

Well, lo and behold, as soon as I relaxed and decided I didn't care where the ball went, I began hitting the ball much better and even won a few holes. I was still a day late and a dollar short. I lost the match but I learned a good lesson that day—a lesson I have remembered all my life. I learned what the old golf pro had been telling my dad and me from day one.

Unwanted muscular tension is the number
one enemy of the golf swing.

Remember, everything in golf is backwards. If you try too hard, you'll only get worse. Relax.

Remember as you learn to play this funny ole game—this is a GAME. You're supposed to relax and have fun. Instead of trying too hard, remember that petulant high school boy and don't be like him. Outsmart that ole golf ball and have fun.

The Object of the Game

The object of the game of golf is to strike a golf ball with a golf club from a designated teeing area causing the ball to fall into a distant four and a quarter inch hole in the ground in as few strokes as possible.

You hit the ball and go find it. You hit it again and go find it again. You hit it again as many times as required until you finally knock it into that little hole on the green marked with a flag on a flagpole.

Golf is that easy. Nothin' to it. Simple.

Let's play golf.

Golf Etiquette

Learning how to behave on the golf course is important—very important. Golf, like any sport, has its rules of behavior. If you want folks to invite you to play with them a second time, you'll need to learn how to behave properly.

All beginners should find an experienced golfing friend to take them to play golf the first few times. Be aware that when your friend takes a novice like you to play golf, it's the equivalent of taking a 5-year-old to the supermarket. There's a mountain of literature available to help you learn the basics of golf course etiquette.

Here are a few to get you started:

1. Dress appropriately.
2. Be still and perfectly quiet when a fellow golfer is about to hit their shot.
3. Repair your pitch marks on the green. Ask your golfing friends to show you how to do this. The golf course professionals in the clubhouse will happily sell you a pitch mark repair tool and show you how to use it. The purpose of repairing pitch marks left by golf balls falling out of the heavens and thudding into the soft soil of the green is to prevent you from having a jumpy-lumpy-bumpy surface when you're putting your golf ball towards the hole. Repair Your Pitch Marks. Smooth the green before you leave. You'll be glad everyone did.
4. Be aware of your fellow golfers, including those on other holes. Do your best not to distract them.

5. Play at the appropriate speed. Keep up with the group in front of you. Don't hold up the group behind you. During the busy season there may be a group of golfers on each of the eighteen holes. One slow group can back up the entire course and throw off scheduled tee times. If the ambassador or ranger asks you to speed up, don't be offended. Don't be a smart-a**. Just because you paid your green fee, it doesn't give you the right to play as if your group is the only group on the golf course. Everyone else paid and they deserve a proper pace of play. Get a move on. Keep up with the group in front of you. You don't want to be like a five-year-old in a supermarket, do you?

6. Never, never, never, never, never, never walk on the grass in the line of a fellow golfer's upcoming putt. Never do that. Did I say never set your foot anywhere on the grass near where a fellow golfer is going to putt their ball? Oh my, sometimes one has to take a five-year-old to the golf course, doesn't one?

There are more points of etiquette you'll need to learn. Buy an appropriate book or go to the internet. You'll have more fun when you learn to behave properly on the golf course and your friends will invite you back.

Equipment You Will Need

You'll need your own equipment. Two golfers can't play out of the same bag. That would take too much time.

Beginners don't need the more expensive fitted clubs or even a full set of clubs. Used clubs or an inexpensive beginner set will do nicely.

You'll need:

1. **Golf Clubs and Bag**. I suggest an inexpensive beginner set that will serve you well for the first year or two. The beginner set will have fewer clubs than a full set but that's perfectly ok to begin with.

2. **Golf Balls.** I suggest the most inexpensive golf balls you can find. Buy three or four dozen. Make sure they're all alike. Always use the same brand of golf ball. Mark each ball with a permanent marker to make them easily identifiable as your golf ball when you are on the golf course. If you always play with the same brand of ball and if you mark them, you'll always know which ball is yours. Later on when you're playing by the rules this will become important.

3. **Tee Pegs.** You'll need some long and short tee pegs which every golfer is allowed to use on their first shot from the teeing ground.

4. **Golf Glove.** You may find a golf glove necessary in the summer months when you begin to perspire. My momma told me that horses sweat, men perspire and women glisten. I usually carry four or five golf gloves in my bag. When it's hot and my hands are extra

sweaty I may change gloves every few holes to make certain I have a good grip on the handle of the club. If your hands are cold you can also wear a golf glove in the winter. Occasionally folks will wear a golf glove on both right and left hands but most people just wear a glove on the top hand to maintain a secure grip.

5. **Ball Mark Repair Tool.** Golfers are expected to repair their pitch mark on the golf green. The depression left in the green by your golf ball must be repaired. You can buy the little tool for that purpose at every golf shop. Always carry it in your pocket when you play.

6. **Ball Marker.** From the beginning your goal as a golfer will be to break a hundred. I suggest you use a quarter minted in 1999 to mark your golf ball on the green. When you break a hundred you can change your ball mark quarter appropriately to reflect your new goal. If you shoot a 99 then get you a small sack of quarters minted in 1998 to use as ball markers.

7. **Golf Shoes.** Golf shoes are optional, but be certain you are wearing shoes that do not have cleats or a similar bottom that might damage the golf green. The main use of golf shoes is to give the golfer a firm stance on uneven ground or on damp grass. To begin with most folks will do fine with a comfortable pair of sneakers.

That's about all you're going to need to begin for a while.

Golf Club Names

A pitching wedge is not for pitching

Last century golf clubs had names rather than numbers. In the modern golf bag we retain the original names of only four clubs from those good ole' days. The rest of our clubs we have given modern bland numbers to replace the old colorful names.

The four clubs which retain their old names are:

Driver

Putter

Pitching Wedge

Sand Wedge

In the old days a golfer might have had in his bag:

1. Driver
2. Brassie-the two wood
3. Spoon-the three wood
4. Baffie-four wood
5. Cleek-the driving iron
6. Mashie-the five iron
7. Spade-the six iron
8. Niblick-the nine iron
9. Pitching Niblick-the pitching wedge
10. Putter

In those early days of golf there was no sand wedge. The pitching niblick, or pitching wedge, was the highest lofted club in the bag at about fifty degrees. In 1932, Gene Sarazen, in a machine shop in New Port Ritchie, Florida, invented the sand wedge. It was a club much like our sand wedge today with about fifty-six degrees of loft. Mr. Sarazen kept it hidden in his golf bag during competitions. He was afraid tournament officials would ban both him and his new club as they were wont to do.

The important thing for you to remember is that your modern pitching wedge is not used for pitching—not since the invention of higher lofted clubs. Today many golfers have 3 or 4 clubs in their bag with more loft than the pitching wedge.

Since 1932, and especially in the last couple of decades, the club manufacturers have lowered the loft of the irons. My pitching wedge is 45°. Therefore, when I want to pitch the ball high into the air around the green and make it stop quickly, I use my sand wedge, which is 56°. I do not use my pitching wedge for pitching. This is a bit confusing, isn't it?

I also carry a modern lob wedge which has 60° loft. You can see it would be a silly mistake for me to try to loft the ball high into the air with my 45° pitching wedge when I have a 56° and a 60° club in my bag.

Remember, the club in your bag called a pitching wedge has a name that comes to us from ages past. The modern golfer should technically think of the pitching wedge as their 10 iron—not a club to be used for pitching. The modern pitching wedge is simply the next club in the series of clubs after the 9 iron. The pitching wedge has about 4° more loft than the nine iron.

Use your sand wedge or lob wedge for pitching the ball high into the air and stopping it quickly around the green. Use your pitching wedge for a full shot from the fairway when a nine iron would hit the ball too far.

No Bifocals

For best results the golfer who uses corrective lenses must use a single lens for distance vision. No professional golf instructor would recommend wearing readers or distance glasses which include readers when setting up to hit a golf ball.

No bifocals, trifocals, or progressives on the golf course—None, Nada, Zilch, Zero, Naught, Zippo. Don't wear 'em when you're hitting golf balls. Readers are for the library and for reading the menu in a restaurant. Readers are not to be worn while striking a golf ball.

Here's why. At address, when the golfer's head is in the correct position, bifocals, trifocals or progressives will distort the golfer's vision of the golf ball lying at the golfer's feet. When viewing the golf ball at address, the golfer's head must be up above the shoulder turn to allow the lead shoulder to turn under the golfer's chin.

Therefore, since the golfer must hold her/his head up high, the golfer looks down at the golf ball through the bottom part of a corrective lens. Bifocals, trifocals and progressives distort the golfer's view of the golf ball—oh dear.

Golfers who insist on wearing corrective lenses with bifocals, trifocals or progressive lenses when they play golf will tend to lower their chin at address in order to see the golf ball through the top part of the corrective lens. That lowering of the golfer's chin and head at address puts the golfer's head in a terrible position for ball striking—a position from which they can never achieve their best results.

Do you want to be a good ball striker? Do you want to hold your head in the best position for consistent ball striking? Then you want your head and chin up above the shoulder turn. The golfer's head should be UP.

The shoulder on the target side of the golfer's body should turn UNDER the golfer's chin on the backswing. It wouldn't be good if your shoulder hit you in the side of the face as you take the club away from the ball, would it?

If you wear corrective lenses when you play golf, make certain they are single lens distance prescription only which will allow you to hold your head UP and have a clear view of the ball at your feet. Corrective lenses must not include a reader lens.

Am I repeating myself?

It's not a good thing when the golfer's shoulder turns into the side of the golfer's face on the backswing. Therefore, telling someone to keep their head down is the absolute worst advice in golf. Unfortunately, it's the most common piece of advice among amateurs—and the worst advice. The golfer's head must be up, up, UP.

The golfer's spine must be straight enough for the head and chin to be UP above the shoulder turn. If the golfer's head is drooping down between the shoulders, the left shoulder will crash into the side of the golfer's face in the middle of the backswing. This crash of the shoulder into the side of the face at the worst possible moment makes consistent ball striking impossible.

If you wear corrective lenses, my advice is go to your eye professional and ask for a single lens distance prescription.

Do not try to play golf while wearing reading glasses.

Next Time You're Sick

No one should do this but let me make a point. Let's say for argument's sake that the next time you get sick you go up and down your street and knock on every door. You ask each of your neighbors if you can have their old prescriptions left over from the last time they were sick. You take home your sack full of your neighbor's old prescription bottles. You sit down with a glass of water and take a pill from each bottle. That would cure you, right?

Nope. No one would do that. Everyone knows that's a stupid thing to do. No one has ever done that in the history of the world.

Golf is the same. You can't take the same golf medicine others take. Each person needs individual golf instruction. I might tell one student to do this to hit the golf ball better and tell the next student to do the opposite.

You get the point.

Next Time You Go Shopping

Everyone wears different kinds of clothes, shoes and hats, don't they? When I go shopping for clothes I have to hunt and hunt through the maze of racks to find my size and style. When I've found something I think is suitable I have to try it on in the changing room and even then it might not fit.

When I was a boy I dreaded going shopping with my mom for school clothes. She didn't want to buy anything without me trying it on first. She always tried to buy clothes that would last the entire school year. She was a smart mom.

Well, we all wear different size clothes, don't we? Golf instruction is as different for different people as buying clothes.

Do yourself a favor and don't wear your golfing friend's clothes, shoes or golfing advice.

Take professional golf lessons to make sure your golfing advice fits as well as your shirt and shoes. You would look funny if you borrowed your neighbor's clothes to wear to the golf course, wouldn't you?

Look at the Pictures
Cut out the pictures and throw away the words

This is my advice as you begin to learn to play golf. Purchase half a dozen golf magazines. Get some for professional male and female golfers. I especially like the photographs of the female professional golfers when studying proper setup because the female professionals aren't required to wear baggy trousers which hide their lower body setup.

Cut out the photographs showing how the professionals use their body to strike a golf ball.

My Daddy gave me his old folder full of pictures he cut out of old magazines over the years. I can't tell you how nostalgic looking at the old photographs of all those famous golfers from my youth. Things change, don't they?

Look at the professionals in the magazines:
1. Notice how their hold the club—the grip.
2. Notice how they hold their arms.
3. Notice how they set their body posture when in the address position.
4. Notice the spine, the position of their watermelon (their behind), their cantaloupe (their head).
5. Notice the ball position.
6. Learn as much as you can from the pictures.

Don't read the words. Imitate the pictures. You have a body configured exactly the same as the professionals. Imitate what you see in the photographs. Get used to it. Before long your professional looking set up will become COMFORTABLE.

How to Learn to Play Golf

The best way to learn to play golf is to take a few professional golf lessons at the very beginning of your golfing career. If new golfers will take a few professional lessons before they begin to play, they will avoid developing some of the worst habits. They'll learn to play better, faster and enjoy the game more.

You'll hear me say this often:

You can't get on the wrong bus
and get to the right place.

For best results, take a professional golf lesson or two when you first begin to play to make sure you get on the right bus.

Get on the Right Bus

Let's say you win a 7-day, all expenses paid vacation at the most expensive resort in Key West. You're a lucky-ducky, aren't you? They promise in their brochures that one day you'll fish for the big ones that you only find way out and deep in the gulf stream. The next day you'll take a sunset sail on a forty-foot ketch and the next day you'll snorkel on a magical reef with a twilight barbeque on the beach. Oh my, what a vacation. Not only did you win this vacation but even free bus transportation is included down to Key West.

You arrive packed and ready. You're confused. You've found two different buses parked there. Which is the right bus? One bus says KEY WEST EXPRESS. The other bus says HAHIRA, GA.

Does it matter which bus you choose? Do you want to spend seven all-expenses-paid days in Hahira, Georgia, population 2,328 or do you want your week in Key West?

Does it matter which bus you get on? Of course it matters.

You can't get on the wrong bus
and get to the right place.

In this little book I'm going to tell you some things about striking a golf ball that I've learned in a lifetime of playing and teaching.

If you want to have fun in Key West, get on the right bus.

Golf - Three Games in One

Putting - Short Game - Long Game

The game of golf can be thought of as three games in one.

1. *Putting*—the game on the green.
2. *Short Game*—Part shots—within seventy yards of the green executed with a partial swing.
3. *Long Game*—Full shots—seventy yards and farther. Shots executed with a full swing.

Putting is the game on and very close around the green when the golfer uses the putter and rolls the ball along the ground.

The Short Game is that part of the golfer's game in which the golfer is so close to the green there is no club in the bag that can be hit with a full swing. The short game means the golfer doesn't hit a full shot—the golfer hits the golf ball with a partial swing—not a full swing. Distance control for part shots around the green is managed by shortening the length of backswing.

The Long Game is that part of the golfer's game in which the golfer takes a full swing.

A few things about the
Setup.

More later

First - The Grip

The grip—by far the number one fundamental

Your good grip
will *FORCE* your body to swing correctly.

Your bad grip
will *PREVENT* your body from swinging correctly.

You can't get on the wrong bus and get to the right place.

In 2008 there was a Monday playoff for the US Open at Torry Pines between Rocco Mediate and Tiger Woods. Rocco held off the famous Tiger Woods and came within a hair's breadth of winning.

In Rocco's book, *Are You Kidding Me*, he tells how he was number one on his high school golf team but wasn't outstanding. He could only break 80 occasionally. Rocco talked his dad into taking him for golf lessons with a well-known local professional, Jim Ferree, in order to make a college golf team. Rocco wanted to play college golf.

After the professional watched Rocco hit a few balls he said wryly, "Son, you have a good swing, but your hands on the club look like two crabs fightin' on a stick."

The very first thing the pro taught Rocco was how to hold the golf club correctly. No golfer can reach their potential with a poor grip. Every golf teacher in the world knows you must hold the club correctly in order to swing correctly.

28

You can't get on the wrong bus and get to the right place.

The professional knew it would be useless to try to teach Rocco to be a good ball striker unless he held the club correctly.

I'm telling you the same thing here in this book. If you get one thing from this book, learn how to hold the golf club properly.

Rocco got his wish. He improved his game and made the golf team at Florida Southern College. Rocco, along with Lee Janzen, helped Florida Southern to the 1985 Division II College championship. And almost 6 years to the day when Mr. Mediate learned his hands looked like two crabs fighten' on a stick, Rocco Mediate played his first tournament on the PGA Tour.

Here's how to hold the golf club:

1. Hold the golf club as far down in your fingers as you can—not in the palm of your hand. For right handed golfers, place the left hand above the right hand on the handle of the golf club.
2. Hold the golf club like you would a fly swatter. Try this: Hold an old-fashioned fly swatter in your right hand. Swat a few imaginary flies on the kitchen counter. Look down at the back of your hand as you hold the deceased fly on the counter with the business end of your swatter. Your right hand holds the golf club the same way as the fly swatter.
3. When you look down at your good golf grip you should be looking at the backs of your hands—not your palms or the inside of your wrists. You shouldn't see your radial arteries on the inside of your wrists. Ask a nurse to show you your radial arteries.
4. The left thumb runs down the top of the shaft and points at the club head.
5. Totally cover your left thumb with your right palm. Imagine the left thumb is a hotdog as it lays on the

handle of the golf club. Imagine your right hand is the upside-down hotdog bun. Put the upside-down bun on top of the hot dog. The ENDS of the fingers of the right hand hold the golf club. Now you're holding your golf club with both hands and your hot dog is securely held UNDER and in the palm of the right hand. Your hot dog will be upside down but that's ok in this case, isn't it?

6. Hold the club as close to the fingertips as possible. Not in the palm of the hand.

7. In the address position, be able to see at least two of the big knuckles on the back of both hands—the big knuckles where your fingers join onto your hand. If you were to open your fingers while holding the golf club without moving your hands, your palms would be facing DOWN.

8. Completely cover the left thumb with the right palm. Have I already said that once? If your left thumb were painted bright orange you couldn't see your colorful left thumb—not one bit of it.

9. Hold the club tight—at least 7 out of 10 on the tightness scale. The golfer must have a constant grip pressure throughout the swing. Sloppy, inconsistent or weak grip pressure is a big no-no.

You may not like holding the club this way to begin with. Everyone I ask to hold the club this way says it feels uncomfortable, but if you don't hold the club this way your hands will look like two crabs fightin' on a stick when you try to hit a golf ball.

You can trust Ben Hogan, Sam Snead, Arnold Palmer, Tiger Woods and the rest of the professionals on both the male and female tours.

The biggest mistake beginners make with the grip is holding the right hand under the club and exposing the left thumb to view. Get the right hand on top and cover that left thumb—put the hot dog in the upside-down hot dog bun.

Ben Hogan, in his famous book *Five Lessons,* takes the first 19 pages to discuss the grip. Study those first nineteen pages and Mr. Hogan's drawings that concern only the grip. Make your hands and fingers look exactly like Mr. Hogan's looked in the drawings. Mr. Hogan makes it clear. How a golfer puts their hands and fingers on the handle of the golf club is the single most important determining factor in the future success of any golfer. Do yourself a favor and purchase the book.

Mr. Hogan makes it clear. There isn't any sense in going to chapter two if you skip chapter one. If you can't hold the golf club correctly you'll be on the wrong bus and spend your entire golf vacation in Hahira, Georgia.

Sam Snead said if folks took as little care with how they held their knife and fork as they did with their grip on the golf club, they would starve to death.

Hold the club correctly and the muscles of your entire body work in concert just like a Beethoven symphony.

Hold the club incorrectly and the muscles of your body don't know what to do or when to do it. Hold the golf club any old way and the music your body makes when striking a golf ball will sound more like a bunch of cats fightin' in the alley.

Get a Grip. Get a good grip.

When Arnold Palmer was about three years of age his dad gave him his first little cut-down golf club. Arnie said he remembers the moment vividly. His dad, who was both greens keeper and club professional in Latrobe, Pennsylvania, gave him the little golf club and showed him how to hold it properly. Mr. Palmer remembers his dad making a big deal out of his grip on the handle of his first little golf club. Arnie's dad placed his son's hands on the handle of the club correctly and then told young Arnie to look down at his hands and fingers and memorize what he saw. His father told him to never change the way you hold the golf club. Never change your grip from what you see now, his dad told him.

Mr. Palmer never did change his grip and aren't we glad.

Arnie's dad, Ben Hogan, Sam Snead, Tiger Woods, Rory McIlroy and every other successful golfer knows the centerpiece of any golf swing is a proper grip which allows all the muscles of the hands, arms, shoulders, torso and legs to operate properly when they strike a golf ball.

You can't get on the wrong bus and get to the right place.

If you make your hands and fingers look like Mr. Hogan's, I personally guarantee you'll be a decent golfer.

However, if you enjoy being the shortest hitter in the group, playing out of the rough, paying out money in the clubhouse after every round and wondering why you can't be more consistent, then hold the club any old way. Go ahead and get on any old bus. Do they have a golf resort in Hahira?

But that's not what I want for you. I want you to hold the club like Mr. Palmer, Mr. Snead, Mr. Hogan, Tiger Woods and Rocco Mediate—so get a grip. Hold the club like those two did.

Second - Set the Club to the Ball

Take your grip
then set the club head behind the ball.

First – Grip the club correctly.
Second – Set the club head squarely behind the ball.

You can't set your body first and then set the club. If you set your body first how would you know where to put your feet? How would you know where to stand? You can't set your car seat unless you're sitting in the seat. You can't reach through the open car door and set your seat and then get in. You could never adjust your car seat correctly that way, could you? You can't set your body to hit a golf ball unless the golf club is first set directly behind the golf ball—as if it were set in concrete. You set the club to the ball AND THEN set your body to the club.

The correctly positioned golf club tells the golfer where to put his body—especially the feet.

Third – Set Your Body to the Club

First – Grip the club correctly.
Second – Set the club head behind the ball.
Third – Set your body to the club.

Golfers stand sideways to the intended line of flight. Everyone usually gets this. The golfer's feet, hips and shoulders should be perpendicular to the intended line of flight.

The most important of these is the shoulders.

If a golfer were to lay a rod against the shoulder joints when standing in the address position, the rod would point at the target—and the rod would be parallel to the intended line of flight.

Fourth – Align Your Body Properly

First – Grip correctly.
Second – Set the club head behind the ball.
Third – Set your body to the club.
Fourth – Align your body to your intended line of flight.

Whether you're on the green putting, hitting a seven iron straight towards the flag or hitting your driver down a wide fairway you should set the club first—and then set your body to the club.

Never, never, never set your feet and your body and then set the club head behind the ball.

First, set the club behind the ball where you want it. Set the club head before you set your feet and body.

Then, when you have a good grip, you have set the club properly and you have set your feet—then you can make certain your shoulders are parallel to the intended line of flight.

The golfer will be properly aligned when his shoulders are parallel to the intended line of flight. Most right-handed beginners will incorrectly align their shoulders well to the left of the target.

The target line and the shoulder line should be parallel.

The
Short Game

What is the Short Game?

Golf shots with less than a full swing.

The short game includes: Pitching, Chipping and Putting.

The short game is used when a golfer is so close to the green they must use a 'part shot' with a partial backswing rather than a 'full shot' with full backswing.

What is a 'Part Shot'?

When the golfer swings and only uses part of a golf swing, not a full backswing with full strength, that's a Part Shot.

The short game is when the golfer employs only part of the power that could be used to hit the golf ball because full power would cause the ball to go over the green and through the woods all the way to grandma's house—not good.

When the golfer is close to the green the golfer must use only part of their power in their swing.

For example: Most golfers will have a sand wedge in their bag. The sand wedge usually has about 56° loft. This is usually the most lofted club in the bag and therefore the club that hits the ball the shortest distance of all the clubs. Most male and many female beginners can hit the golf ball 70 yards with a full swing sand wedge.

Therefore, any shot less than 70 yards attempted with a sand wedge must be struck with a partial backswing—not a full backswing.

Thus, all shots within a certain range for any given golfer will be part shots. This 'Short Game' composed of partial swings is played a bit differently than the long game.

Short Game and Club Head Speed

When the golfer is around the green and playing a part shot he/she is not taking a full swing at the golf ball. Even though the golfer is not swinging with a full backswing, the club head must be on the increase of speed on the downswing and at impact. The impact must be crisp. In other words, the golf club cannot slow down or coast into the golf ball.

Coasting into the golf ball with a club head that is slowing is like driving a car down a hill on ice. The driver has no control. A golfer who lets the club head coast into impact will have no control of the golf club.

Coasting into any shot puts the golfer's muscles into neutral. They don't work. The club head must be on the increase of speed when it strikes the golf ball—even for a short putt, chip, or pitch. Think of driving a big nail with a big hammer into a big piece of wood. You would do that with a big hard swing. Right?

Now imagine a small hammer and a small nail and a small piece of wood. You still have to hit the nail with the hammerhead on the increase of speed—the little hammer with its little, short backswing still has to hit the little nail head with a crisp contact. The little hammer delivers a much shorter stroke than the big hammer but it's still a sharp swing and crisp contact with the nail head.

In the short game with part shots the golfer takes a shorter backswing but the golfer still has to hit the ball sharply.

You can't coast into a putt, chip or pitch—or any shot.

Remember—around the green with part shots the club head must be on the increase of speed at impact. That will mean a shorter backswing for a short shot—a longer backswing to make the ball go farther.

Learning to hit part shots around the green has no magic formula. Get good instruction. Learn the proper set up and then PRACTICE. Only around the practice green will a golfer develop the feel necessary to have a good short game.

Distance Control in the Short Game

The backswing is the key with Part Shots.

What does the golfer do when a full swing with any club in the bag will hit the ball too far? How do we hit the shorter part shots when we're closer to the green?

This is simple. Just as the position of the accelerator in an automobile determines how fast or slow the car travels, the length of the backswing determines how far the golfer hits the golf ball. If you want the ball to go the maximum distance for any club in your bag, you must use a full swing with a full backswing.

The golfer shouldn't think of hitting the ball harder or easier. A full backswing gives the golfer maximum distance with any given club.

For part shots the golfer controls distance by length of backswing.

Reducing the length of backswing will correspondingly reduce the distance the ball travels.

The golfer should never think of hitting the golf ball 'easier' or 'harder' to control distance. Distance is a direct result of a shorter or longer backswing.

Remember, a part-shot is a stroke used by a golfer to hit a ball less than the full distance.

For example: A golfer may hit their 56° sand wedge 80 yards with a full swing. That same golfer may be forced into a position where they have only 50 yards to the flag but they must go over an intervening hazard. They need the sand wedge for loft in order to hit the ball high but they know they can't swing with a full backswing or the ball would go 80 yards—30 yards too far.

What should they do?

A wise golfer with have practiced with their sand wedge and know that if they reduce the length of their backswing a certain amount they can hit the ball the required 50 yards and stop the ball on the green.

Shorten the backswing for a shorter distance. With the shorter backswing the golfer can still swing through impact with the club head on the increase of speed.

Taking a too long backswing means the unfortunate golfer will be required to slow the head of the golf club before impact which will always give a bad result.

The club head, even on part shots, must be on the increase of speed at impact. The wise golfer will control distance by reducing the length of the backswing—not by speeding up or slowing down the swing.

The wise golfer will never think of reducing the distance they're going to send the golf ball by simply thinking they will hit the ball easier.

A wise golfer doesn't hit the ball easier or harder. A wise golfer controls distance by developing one smooth swing and changing length of backswing to control distance with the part shots around the green.

Putting - Stance and Set-up

Remember earlier when I said the golf game is divided into three games? Of course you do. The golfer will set up in putting a little differently than the other two parts of the golf game because with a putter the golfer is stroking a short shot and using little energy.

The golfer's set-up on the green with a putter is slightly different than the set-up for hitting a 7-iron approach into the green or a high, beautiful 5 wood.

When the golfer is putting on the golf green:

1. Feet should be shoulder width.
2. Most of the weight on the heels. The weight on the heels stabilizes the body. The fewer moving parts when putting, the better.
3. I suggest beginners learn to grip the club differently for putting than for all the rest of the shots in golf. I suggest left hand low on the putter. In the old days we called it 'cross-handed' putting. Normally a right-hand golfer will have the left hand at the top of the handle and the right hand below the left. I believe most golfers will get better results when they putt if they use left hand low on the handle of the putter. This 'crosshanded' style of putting helps reduce the unwanted snap of the wrists at the moment of impact—thus fewer moving parts and more control.
4. Grip down on the putter handle. Make the putter shorter for better control.
5. In the stance, place the ball slightly left of center.

6. Eliminate wrist movement in the putting stroke. I've been using left hand low for several years. It still feels strange, but I'm a much better putter because left hand low takes most of my unwanted and unnecessary wrist action out of my putting stroke.
7. Use the shortest backswing of the putter possible to strike the golf ball hard enough to get it to the hole. You cannot coast your putter head into impact and expect to control distance or line.
8. The golfer's head should be perfectly stationary during the putting stroke for best results. If the golfer is swaying left and right during the putting stroke it's a recipe for a broken heart.

Note: I use left hand low on shorter putts—putts less than 40 feet. I use right hand low/left hand high on my putts when they get somewhere around 40 feet and longer. When I have to give the ball a good rap with my putter I go back to the same grip I would use if I were chipping or pitching—left hand high.

First – Really Short Putts

You know how to grip the putter. You know how to stand. Here's how to begin to learn to putt.

1. Take your putter and one ball to the practice green.
2. Find a hole that is on flat ground.
3. Lay the ball down 4 inches from the hole.
4. Address the ball and take your putting stance.
5. Stroke the ball into the cup with your putter.

You just made your first putt—a hole in one. Isn't this game easy?

Then lay another ball down 6 inches from the hole and do the same. Then go to12 inches.

You're beginning at the hole and learning to play golf backwards towards the tee box. The object of the game is to get the golf ball into that 4¼ inch hole in as few strokes as possible.

First, learn to make those short putts no longer than 6 inches before you begin putting from 12 inches.

After you have learned to putt the ball into the hole from close distances then you can learn to putt from longer distances.

Important note: When you're putting from longer distances make certain the ball stops close to the hole if it doesn't fall in. We don't want a long second putt, do we? We want that second putt to be a short tap-in, don't we? We never want to take more than two putts on any green.

Second – Longer Putts

Stop the ball beside the hole if you miss your putt.

With the ball 3 feet from the hole, practice putting and stopping the ball within a hole's width of the cup if the ball doesn't fall into the hole. The cup is 4¼ inches wide. When you putt, learn to control your speed by stopping the ball very close to the hole if it doesn't drop into the cup.

If you learn to stop the ball very close to the hole you'll never take more than two putts and you'll discover a healthy percentage of the first putts will fall in.

When you can stop the ball a hole's width from the cup from 6 and 8 feet you will be one of the best putters on your block. Trust me.

Finally learn to putt to the hole from all over the green. Be a hula-hoop putter from longer distances.

When you're on the green but far from the hole, imagine there's a hula-hoop around the hole. Learn to lag the ball close to the hole so that your golf ball stops inside of your imaginary hula-hoop. Learn to use gravity's pull on the golf ball on unlevel greens to your advantage. Use the slopes, hills and valleys around the green to help you get the ball close to the hole inside your imaginary hula-hoop.

Each time you play arrive 15 minutes early and practice your putting. Putting is the most important part of golf. Most of your practice should be on the short game.

I believe you can do this—because you can.

45

Reading Potato Chip Greens

A few years ago I heard a woman complaining about a new golf course in our area. She said the new undulating greens were so up and down they reminded her of large potato chips. I still laugh when I recall her remark. Her unique description of golf greens was accurate.

You have probably discovered that golf greens are not perfectly level like a pool table. Here is a simple way to learn to determine the path of the golf ball when your find yourself on an undulating putting surface that looks like a monster potato chip.

1. Go to your practice putting green.
2. Take 4 golf balls and no putter.
3. Go to a spot on the green with 4 balls and no golf club.
4. Pick out a target on the green thirty or forty feet away.
5. Roll the ball softly and slowly underhanded like a bowling ball towards your target.
6. Watch the golf ball as it travels slowly over the uneven surface.
7. Notice how the ball follows the contour of the ground.
8. Notice how the unlevel green makes the ball bend left and right.

I don't recommend golfers use their putter to do this because practicing with a putter would require the golfer to look up quickly after the stroke to see what the ball is doing.

It's important to keep a steady head and torso during the putting stroke and NOT look up quickly with a jerk—therefore in this drill we roll the ball underhanded rather than using a putter. Using a putter with this drill, rather than rolling the ball by hand, would teach the golfer a bad habit.

Rolling the ball softly underhand and watching how it travels will teach you how to predict the golf ball's roll on uneven potato chip greens.

Rolling the golf ball underhand on a golf green without a putter is a good way to practice reading greens. You'll learn a lot about how gravity pulls the golf ball downhill in a predictable curve and then on your way home you can pick up a big bag of potato chips.

Third Putt from off the Green

Use your putter from off the green when you can.

First, learn to putt from short distances.
Second, learn to putt from longer distances.
Third, putt from off the green.

The wise golfer can and should use their putter even when they're not on the green. The smart golfer will use their putter when they're not on the green when favorable ground conditions permit.

Learn to putt from the fringe and make the ball stop close to the hole. When I was a boy they used to call the fringe the frog-hair, but I don't hear it called that much anymore.

The putter is your best friend when your ball is off the green. From off the green you'll make far fewer mistakes with your putter than with any lofted club.

Learn to roll the ball along the ground with your putter when you can. No matter where your ball might end up around the green, learn to get it close to the hole on the next shot by using just your putter. It's fun. Each time you play, go to the practice green and practice with your putter for at least ten minutes.

Finally, go way off the green with only your putter. Go 10, 20 or 30 yards away from the edge of the green.

Use your putter and one ball. See how close you can get the ball to the hole.

Practice putting from way off the green.

Learn what you can and cannot do with your putter.

Learning what you can't do with your putter is just as important as learning what you can do with your putter. Most people never learn to use their putter from way off the green as they should. They begin using lofted clubs like a pitching wedge instead of the putter.

Using lofted clubs close to the green require a far greater skill level than using the putter.

Beginning golfers should only use a lofted club around the green when it's impossible to use the putter. Lofted clubs should only be used around the green when you cannot putt.

When you learn what your putter can and cannot do, you can take that skill to the golf course. When ground conditions permit, you can roll the ball with your putter even though you are 20, 30 or 40 yards or more from the green.

Other times you may have a shot with long grass between you and green. From your practice with the putter you will have learned that long grass makes it impossible to roll the ball using your putter. The long grass makes putting unpredictable.

When you're practicing around the green it's a good idea to practice exactly what you are going to do when you play. Take one ball and your putter. Practice getting up and down from around the green. Every time you play you will have access to a practice green right by the clubhouse or the first tee. Take one ball and your putter and spend at least 5 minutes from off the green.

Even after you learn to use lofted clubs successfully around the green continue to practice shots with your putter from well off the green. Keep that skill honed.

You'll make fewer mistakes around the green with your putter than with your lofted clubs.

Each time I give a playing lesson I teach the student to use their putter from off the green when ground conditions warrant. They're always amazed how close they're able to get the ball to the hole.

You will find when you're off the green that you'll get the ball closer to the hole with your putter than with any lofted club when ground conditions permit.

Your worst putt from off the green will end up closer to the hole than your best attempt with a lofted club.

What do you do if you decide you can't putt successfully? In that case you must hit your ball in such a way that it hops over the unpredictable ground conditions. Using a lofted club, like a 7 iron, to hit a low shot that will hop over unpredictable ground conditions and then roll towards the flag is called 'chipping'. Hitting a high arching shot that stops quickly is called 'pitching'. Putting from off the green is called 'SMART' golf.

Putting from WAY off the Green

If you want to be a better than average short game player, learn to putt from long distances off the green.

When we were children playing out in the yard we threw, kicked and rolled things along the ground. Even after all these years we adults still have stored in our mind the mounds of motor data gathered when we were children necessary to help us propel an object laterally along the ground—such as a golf ball.

1. Go to your practice green.
2. Take 5 balls and go 5 yards off the putting surface and putt to a hole.
3. Then go 10 yards off the putting surface and hit your 5 balls.
4. Then go up to 20 yards off the green and practice putting—then 30 yards and even 40 yards. Have fun.
5. Learn what you can and cannot do with your putter when you're not on the green.
6. Learn when you can use your putter successfully—learn when you can't use your putter.
7. Because of your experience around the practice putting green you'll learn when ground conditions make putting unpredictable.
8. When you cannot putt because of unpredictable ground conditions you'll have to chip.
9. When you can't chip, you'll have to pitch.

Even a small amount of practice with your putter will teach you how easy it is to get the ball close to the pin by rolling the ball along the ground as opposed to flying it through the air. Rolling the ball with your putter is an excellent way to get the ball close to the hole if ground conditions allow. You'll be amazed. Flying the ball through the air is a more difficult shot but sometimes we're forced to do so by unpredictable ground conditions.

If you practice from off the green with your putter:
1. You'll learn when you can and cannot putt from off the green.
2. You'll become an expert on assessing ground conditions.
3. You'll learn when ground conditions allow and when ground conditions prohibit the use of a putter.
4. You'll learn when you can use your putter and when you are forced by unpredictable ground conditions to use a lofted club and fly over the difficulty.

What do you do when unpredictable ground conditions prevent you using your putter?

You'll grip down on a 7 iron and use it much like a putter to make the ball hop over the unpredictable ground conditions. The 7 iron will hit a low shot that spends a little time in the air and long time on the ground rolling to the flag.

What have we learned?

If you want to be a good short game player the first thing you need to learn is how to putt from off the green when you can.

Learn to be a good judge of ground conditions so you will know when you can putt successfully and when putting from off the green just won't work.

Why is putting from off the green your first choice?

Because using the putter when you're off the green is easier.

Why is the putter easier?

Because you don't have to take a divot or hit the soil with the putter. That makes sense doesn't it?

If you chip (a low running shot) or pitch (a high lofted shot that stops quickly) you must hit the soil with the bottom of those clubs. When you putt from off the green you don't have to hit the soil with the bottom of the putter. How good is that?

One last piece of advice. Because your putter has no loft, you need to play the ball forward in your stance towards your left foot when putting from off the green. This helps get the ball up on top of the grass immediately and rolling smoothly towards the target.

If you play the ball back in your stance when putting from off the green you'll be driving the ball down into the grass and the golf ball will tend to hop giving unpredictable results.

For long shots from off the green with your putter I recommend you hold the putter exactly as you would hold any iron on any approach shot (not left-hand low as with shorter putts on the green). When you are putting from off the green use the same grip you would use if you were chipping or hitting a full eight iron.

Practice putting from off the green regularly. Learn what you can and cannot do with a putter from off the green. If you do, you'll discover the rest of your short game will improve dramatically.

Chip When You Can't Putt

Putt when you can.
Chip only when you can't putt.

What is a chip shot?

A chip shot is a part-shot. Unlike a putt, a chip shot hops over unpredictable ground conditions. A chip shot travels for a short time through the air barely above ground level and then rolls. It's a low shot. A chip shot is a knee high or lower shot. A chip shot never goes high. A chip spends more time on the ground rolling than in the air. A chip behaves much like a putt.

Chip with your 7 iron. You'll hit the ball with your 7 iron with almost the exact same lateral force you would use if you were using your putter from that same distance. That's why you need to become proficient with your putter from off the green. Putting from off the green and chipping from off the green are brother and sister. You'll use practically the same amount of force with both swings.

The set up for a chip shot is different from the set up for a putt because of the difference in the loft of the two clubs. The 7 iron has a good bit of loft. The putter no loft.

If you know how hard to swing your putter from off the green to get the ball close to the hole, you already know how much force to use to chip from off the green. The two shots are brother and sister.

1. A chip shot hops over unpredictable ground conditions and then rolls onto the green.

54

2. A chip shot does not go high into the air. (A short shot high into the air is called a pitch shot).
3. A chip is executed much like a long putt but with a lofted club, usually a 7 or 8 iron.
4. The heavy head and flat bottom of the 7 iron makes it easy to use in the fringe area around the green.
5. You would choose to chip the golf ball when unpredictable ground conditions prohibit the use of the putter.
6. A chip shot hops over unpredictable ground conditions.

Putt when you're on the green.

Putt when you're just off the edge of the green.

Putt when you're way off the green and have predictable ground conditions between you and the pin.

Why use the putter from way off the green? In your short game, you'll find you'll get better results around the green with a putter than with any other club when ground conditions allow.

But what if you can't putt? What if the grass is too high? What if the grass is wet with dew or rain? What if there is a big root in the way? What if there is an intervening ground condition that prevents the ball from rolling predictably? What if there are sticks, twigs and odd little mounds of earth that make a putt that rolls on the ground unreliable?

If you have unpredictable ground conditions use a 7 iron instead of your putter and hop over/fly over the unpredictable ground conditions.

I thought the 7 iron was for long shots into the green from the fairway with a full swing?

By rule golfers are allowed only fourteen clubs in their bag. Therefore, golfers make some clubs do double duty. Experienced golfers can hit a long approach with their 7 iron into the green. Golfers can also use that same 7 iron to hit a knee high chip a short distance and roll the ball up to the flag—a part-shot.

How do you chip with a 7 iron?
1. Use the same grip as you would with your irons.
2. Use the same kind of stroke as with your putter.
3. Grip down the handle of your 7 iron. Grip down so the 7 iron is the same length as your putter. When chipping I always touch the steel shaft of my 7 iron with my right index finger so I can be assured of the exact same balance point every time I chip.
4. Feet very close together—almost touching.
5. Place your right foot perfectly square to the intended line of flight. Point your right toe straight at the golf ball. Thus, your right foot is at a perfect right angle to the target line. Kinda like a T-square would look.
6. Play the ball in front of your right big toe. Point your right big toe at the ball.
7. Stand very close to the ball—no more than 12 or 14 inches from your right big toe.
8. Stand a little more upright than a full-swing shot because you're standing so close.
9. Your hands and arms should actually be touching your clothing. Standing too far from the ball makes your arms unstable and you'll tend to spray the ball.
10. Let the top of the handle of the 7 iron be pointing toward your left shoulder joint in a line with your left arm. This will put your hands in front of the club head and the ball.
11. Have more weight on your left heel than the right.
12. NEVER let the weight transfer to your right leg during the backswing. There is NO WEIGHT SHIFT in chipping. NONE. Your weight is on your left heel

throughout the swing. There is no need for a weight transfer. This is a delicate part-shot. Don't complicate things with weight shift.

13. Use very little wrist action. (no flipping of the wrists)
14. L-o-w to the ground backswing with very little wrist action.
15. Swing through the ball with a smooth stroke (not a jabbing motion). Almost let the club swing itself.
16. Steady head throughout the swing just like the putting action.
17. See the spot under the ball after impact. After you swing through the ball and the ball is on its way, make certain you see the ground where the ball was. This will insure you keep a steady head throughout.
18. You will strike the ball with a downward blow because you're playing the golf ball on the right side of your stance in front of your right toe. (if the ball was on the left side of your stance you would tend to contact the ball on the upswing)
19. The bottom of the club will go through the ball and down into the grass to the soil—this is why using the putter from off the green is easier than chipping. The putter doesn't contact the soil.
20. Keep the backswing low to the ground. Then keep the follow-through low to the ground also.

WARNING-Any attempt to help the ball into the air with an upward, scooping-flipping motion of the club head will be bad—very bad—really bad. Scooping is excellent for ice cream but dreadful for chipping.

Putt when you can.

Chip only when you cannot putt.

Putting from off the green when ground conditions permit will yield better results than chipping. Your worst putt from off the green will often be closer to the flag than your playing partner's best chip.

Chip ONLY when you can't putt.

Pitch When You Can't Chip

Putt from off the green when you can.
Chip when you can't putt.
Pitch only when you can't putt or chip.

What is pitching? Pitching is a high arching lob shot that stops quickly when it hits the ground. The pitch shot spends more time in the air than on the ground in contrast to the chip shot—which spends more time on the ground rolling than in the air.

When should you pitch?
You should pitch only when you can't putt or chip.

Why?
Because pitching is more difficult than chipping or putting.

Putting and chipping from off the green will always get you closer to the hole than pitching. Always choose putting and chipping over pitching if ground conditions allow. Putting and chipping are brother and sister. They get along well. Pitching is a 4th cousin twice removed. A successful pitch shot is more difficult to execute than a putt or a chip. Pitching requires a higher level of skill.

A pitch is a high trajectory shot that spends more time in the air than on the ground and stops quickly. Pitching should be the amateur's very last choice. It is the most difficult shot to hit and control around the green.

When should you use a pitch shot?

The golfer should pitch when faced with a shot around the green over an intervening hazard, such as a sand trap, that requires the ball to stop quickly. A pitch shot requires a high trajectory shot from a highly lofted club.

Which club should you use when pitching?

You should choose your highest lofted club in your bag for pitching. A sand wedge has about 56° loft. Some golfers will also carry a lob wedge which has 60°.

I'm often asked the question:

"Why don't I use the pitching wedge for pitching?"

The modern pitching wedge is not the correct club to be used for pitching. The club labeled P or PW is simply the 10 iron in the series of numbered irons. The modern pitching wedge is usually about 45° loft as opposed to the sand wedge with 56° loft or the lob wedge with 60°. Pitching wedge is the pre 1932 name for the club with the highest loft in the golfer's bag.

Back then you would use your pitching wedge for a pitch shot because there was no sand wedge or lob wedge. Today if you have a pitch shot around the green you should use your sand wedge because it has the most loft. Never use your pitching wedge. The sand wedge has about 12° more loft than the pitching wedge.

Before 1932 the highest lofted club in the golfer's bag was a pitching wedge with about 50 degrees loft. In 1931 Gene Sarazen invented the sand wedge in a machine shop in New Port Ritchie, Florida. His creation was a club of about 56° loft with a wider sole that would make it easier for him to hit high lofted pitch shots around the green and come out of sand with more accuracy.

He began using it in 1932. However, some say that Horton Smith used a sand wedge in 1930 and gave one to Bobby Jones to use that year. In any case, the inventive Sarazen kept his new sand wedge covered in his bag in the early days for fear tournament officials would ban his new club.

It's interesting to note that over the years club manufacturers have lowered the club lofts substantially from Gene Sarazen's day. I gave a lesson to a lady recently who had a pitching wedge with only 36° loft—a 6 or 7 iron in the old days.

If you want to hit a shot high into the air that will stop quickly you should use the highest lofted club in your bag which will be the sand wedge and not the pitching wedge.

How do I hit a pitch shot?

When you pitch, you have chosen a shot in which the bottom of the club MUST hit the soil. The bottom of the club MUST get into the soil below the ball in order for the ball to hit the center of the very large face of the sand wedge.

To execute this shot you should have a lie with at least a little grass under the ball. If you have a tight lie around the green you probably won't choose to pitch the ball.

Here's how to play the pitch shot:

1. Play the ball slightly back in your stance—towards your back foot. Never towards the front foot. When you hit a pitch shot the club head must still be on the downward path—never on the upward path. You can't scoop a pitch shot.
2. Grip the club normally. Don't grip down the handle like a chip shot with a 7 iron.
3. Swing through the ball making certain the bottom of the club skips off the dirt.
4. The hands and the handle of the club should be in the middle of your body in line with your sternum if you want the ball to go high. (Your hands and the handle of the club *must not* be in front of your left thigh unless you want the ball to go low…that's another shot you'll learn in a year or two).

5. For a full shot your body weight should be symmetrical with weight on your heels.

6. For a less than full shot, lean slightly to your left heel and keep the weight there. There is no weight shift in short shots around the green. (If you shift your weight to your right during the backswing you will hit the ground behind the ball.)

7. When you hit a pitch shot, you should skip the bottom of the club off the ground directly under the ball. Hitting the soil with the bottom of the club head is the important ingredient many fail to include when they attempt to pitch. Try this to understand why this club MUST hit the soil under the ball. Pick the club up vertically with the handle in the air above your head and hold the club head in your hand at eye level. Place a golf ball on the middle of the face of the wedge— right in front of your eyes. Holding the ball in the center of the clubface and with the club head at eye level, notice how much of the club head is BELOW the bottom of the ball. You MUST skip the bottom of the club off the soil in order to hit the ball in the center of the face of the club. You do not want to take a fat divot before you strike the ball. You simply want the club head to skip with effortlessness like skimming a stone on water at the moment of impact. In this case, the soil is the water. Get the bottom of the club down to the soil.

8. One way to insure you don't take a fat divot before you strike the ball is to take a LOW backswing. Take a low backswing and make a low follow through and the club MUST skip off the soil. (take a steep backswing and you'll stick your pick in the ground, won't you?)

9. The ground and grass absorb a very large amount of energy and slow the club head. Therefore, you will have to swing a little harder for a pitch shot than you might expect to because of the extra energy absorbed by the soil and by the vertical trajectory of the ball.

Always putt when you can. If you can't putt, then chip. If you can't putt or chip, then you are forced to pitch. Learn to skip that big bottom of your sand wedge off the soil. That's called pitching.

Set up For
The Long Game

Full Swing Set up

One Swing – 14 Clubs
One swing for all clubs.

The golfer should seek to develop:

One swing,
One swing speed,
One smooth, effortless tempo,
One grip,
One stance,
One backswing,
One finish.

Golfers have fourteen clubs.
Golfers have one consistent swing.
Each of the fourteen clubs has a different loft.
Each club will hit the ball a different distance.
Golfers have one consistent swing.
We don't swing harder or easier to control distance.

From experience golfers choose the correct club for the correct distance. Golfers have one consistent swing.

Aren't you glad to know you don't have one club and fourteen swings? I know I am.

Golf Clubs Must Strike the Soil

"Make the dirt fly," Daddy says.

Ok, you're ready to hit the ball like you've seen the big girls and big boys do on TV. Keep in mind:

> Tennis racquets don't hit the court.
> Baseball bats don't hit the plate.
> Croquet mallets don't take divots.
> Golf clubs are quite different.

Unlike tennis racquets, baseball bats and croquet mallets,

Golf clubs MUST hit the soil at the same moment they strike a golf ball.

Yep, that's right. In order for you to strike the golf ball in the middle of the club face, the bottom of your golf club must hit the soil. We swing down at a golf ball with our irons.

Golf clubs contact the dirt, soil, earth—at the same moment they strike the golf ball. When you're chipping, pitching and hitting full iron shots, the bottom of the golf club must contact the soil. The dirt must fly, as Daddy says.

There are two exceptions. The golfer does not hit the soil with the driver or putter.

Here is a visual that will help you see what you are trying to accomplish.

1. Take a 7 iron in one hand and a golf ball in the other.

2. Hold the head of the 7 iron right in front of your eyes with the handle of the club pointed straight up above your head toward the ceiling.
3. Place and hold a golf ball in the middle of the face of your seven iron—right there in front of your eyes.
4. Notice where the bottom of the club head is in relation to the bottom of the golf ball.
5. Notice how much of the bottom of the club is below the ball when you place the golf ball in the middle of the clubface. You didn't know that, did you?

Obviously, golfers want to strike the golf ball in the middle of the clubface. When a golfer strikes a golf ball lying on the ground the bottom of the club head must go well below the bottom of the golf ball. What is BELOW the golf ball?

The golf club must go INTO the soil. When you watch the big boys and big girls on TV you'll see them hit their approach shots into the green. You'll see them take a big chunk of sod after they hit the golf ball. That's the natural result of striking a golf ball in the center of your clubface with a downward motion of the club head. Obviously, one can't strike a golf ball with an up-swing. If the golf ball is on the ground how could a golfer possibly get the head of the golf club lower than the ball and swing up at it? The only thing lower than the ball is DIRT. Therefore, the golfer MUST swing DOWN in order to hit the golf ball in the middle of the clubface.

If the golfer doesn't hit the soil with the bottom of the club head, the golfer will unintentionally strike the ball with the sharp, thin bottom leading edge of the club head. If you mistakenly hit the golf ball with the bottom leading edge of the golf club instead of hitting the golf ball in the club face where the grooves are, the result will be completely unpredictable. A golf ball hit with the bottom leading edge of the golf club could go anywhere. For predictable results, the golfer must strike the golf ball in the middle of the club head to allow the grooves of the golf club to hold the golf ball on the clubface during impact and give a predictable and happy result.

Note: If you're afraid to hit the soil or if you don't want to take a divot out of the pretty grass you might take up croquet. The croquet folks don't allow you to hit the ground with the croquet mallets and take divots on their beautifully manicured croquet lawns—but then you can't hit a croquet ball high into the air and watch it land on the green, can you?

Feet Flat on the Ground

The golf swing requires a stable table.

Since Daddy and I first began to play golf together, Daddy has been a student of golf and the golf swing. Daddy is a thinker. Over the years he has learned a lot about what constitutes a proper golf swing and what to avoid.

Daddy was having problems he couldn't seem to iron out himself so he decided to take a professional golf lesson. The pro asked Daddy what the problem was.

Daddy replied to the pro's question, "I think I'm jumping at the ball just before I lunge at it."

Daddy would tell me that story every time we discussed the importance of balance and stability during the golf swing. Daddy and I knew we must have a stable table through impact.

If our golf shoes didn't stay flat on the ground until after the club head impacts the golf ball we were in for trouble. At address the golfer wants a strong steady base with the feet flat on the ground with most of the weight on the heels.

Think of the golfer's steady base/stable table this way:

The golfer's body is divided into two parts. The upper body from the waist up is the golfer's hitting machine. The lower body from the waist down is the table that supports the hitting machine above. The golfer's hitting machine rests on the golfer's hitting table. The golfer's hitting table is composed of the big muscles below the waist—the buttocks, the thighs, calves and feet. The lower part of the golfer's body must provide a STABLE PLATFORM for the golfer's hitting machine.

The golfer must have a Stable Table

This steady base provided by the lower body is established at address with the feet and shoes firmly attached to the ground. The stable table must continue through the backswing and downswing until after impact. The golfer's graceful finish position with the back foot off the ground and all the weight on the left foot doesn't occur until AFTER impact.

Consistent ball striking requires a steady, strong, stable base for the golf swing. That steady base is provided by the feet. That's kinda obvious, isn't it? Have I made my point?

The golfer doesn't run, bounce, jump, walk, slide, skate, stagger, skip, hop, slip or slither while striking the ball. During the golf swing the golfer's shoes should be firmly attached to the soil—flat on the ground. There must be a stable table.

Unwanted shifting of weight from the heels to the toes during the golf swing is disastrous. A balanced, stable lower body provides a base for the upper body to turn and swing the golf club at the ball. The stable table begins with feet flat on the ground and the feet stay flat on the ground until after impact with the ball.

That beautiful finish position with the right heel up in the air with only the right toe on the ground doesn't occur until AFTER impact with the golf ball.

If you want to build an excellent golf posture it must begin with a strong stable base—the bottom of your feet. You must have a stable table for consistent ball striking.

Recently I went to a local restaurant to do a little computer work. I set my computer on the table and got connected to their Wi-Fi. I bought me a tall, cold ice tea to sip as I worked. As I sat down with my tall glass of ice tea I leaned on the table top. One of the legs of my table was slightly shorter than the other three. Each time I leaned on the table with my forearm, the table wobbled and threatened to slosh my tea all over my keyboard. I had to take a folded napkin and jam it under the short table leg. I should have checked to see if it was a STABLE TABLE before I sat down with my computer.

You must have a stable table in golf, too. If you are jumping and pirouetting gracefully you might be a good basketball player or a good ballerina, but you won't be a good golfer.

During your golf swing make certain your table is stable. Keep your feet attached to the soil until AFTER impact with the golf ball. Use good golf shoes. Leave your ballerina shoes, your basketball shoes, your baseball shoes and soccer shoes at home.

Grandma's Screen Door

Remember your grandmother's screen door? Remember that round black spring that connected the middle part of the screen door to the doorframe? That spring kept the door shut tight so the flies and mosquitoes couldn't get inside the house in the summer. Remember how if you let the door go when it was wide open it would slam and make a loud noise?

When you open the screen door the spring stretches and builds tension. When you let go of the screen door, the spring slams the door against the door frame and your grandmother shouts at you, doesn't she?

Well, your body during a golf swing works exactly the same way as your grandmother's screen door. The bottom of your shoes are one end of the golf spring. Your hands and golf club are the other end of the spring. The golfer's body twists in the middle between the feet and the hands building tension. This twisting of the muscles of the body stores power. When you open the screen door, the spring stores enough energy to shut the door without any effort. The golf swing works the same way. After the golfer winds up on the backswing, the downswing requires almost no effort.

As the golfer takes the golf club away from the golf ball the golfer's body twists/turns as it builds and stores muscular tension in all the muscles—just like grandma's screen door. The golfer's arms go back and the wrists cock at the top of the backswing storing even more energy. At the top of the backswing the golfer has stored a great amount of energy in his/her body. After the golfer's spring has been wound, the golfer unwinds the muscular spring and hits the ball. Golfers love to watch the golf ball fly long and straight. Don't you love that feeling?

If the golfer's feet move before impact, the golfer has prematurely released the stored tension. If the feet move before impact, power has leaked away. If the golfer's feet spin, lift, twist or hop before impact, it's the same as taking one end of grandma's spring loose from her door frame.

If the end of grandma's spring wasn't attached to the door frame, would the spring work properly? Nope. If one end of grandma's spring was loose, the screen door wouldn't slam shut. If the golfer's feet are moving before impact it makes it impossible to deliver full power.

The golfer builds the tension/power necessary to strike the golf ball by coiling the body on the backswing as the entire body turns away from the ball like a big spring. Since the golfer's feet are firmly attached to the soil, the golfer can maintain that tension all the way to impact if the feet don't move. The stored energy is released when the club head strikes the golf ball. The only parts of the golfer's body to rest against any outside source are the feet. Only the feet touch the ground or anything else. 100% of the golfer's stability comes from the golfer's firm and solid connection with the soil beneath.

The golfer's body is a big spring. When the golfer is coiling his or her spring on the backswing, the golfer's shoes must stay flat on the ground—just like grandma's spring must stay connected to the doorframe. The shoes stay flat and connected to the soil until after impact. The golfer's shoes are one end of the spring—the club the golfer holds is the other end.

When I was a boy I would fly out grandma's screen door on her back porch in the summertime. When I was a boy I think I ran everywhere. I wish I had some of that energy now.

I would be running so fast when I left grandma's house that I wouldn't hear the old door slam until I had reached the end of the driveway. About then I would hear grandma shout at me not to slam the door, but she was much too late. I was long gone and later I could always claim that I was too far away to hear.

If you want to hear that screen door slam once again and watch that 7 iron fly long and straight towards the flag, you can't take one end of the spring loose.

Keep those feet flat on the ground until after impact.

Feet Shoulder Width

The feet should be shoulder width—not one inch more.

The golfer's feet at address should be shoulder width and no more. If the golfer's feet are too far apart the big muscles in the lower body, the gluteus maximus, the back and thighs, will be in a nasty bind.

Here's a test. Stand up at home and imagine you must wait in line for a bus. You must wait thirty minutes on our imaginary bus. Oh no, but don't worry. We'll imagine it's a very nice bus going to a very nice resort, but you can't get out of line or you'll lose your place. You must patiently stand in this line for thirty minutes. You can't walk around. Please humor me and try this.

As you stand still in one spot holding your place in line, allow your body to tell you the most comfortable position for the width of your feet and legs. Let your body tell you how wide apart your feet should be to wait comfortably for this bus with the least amount of discomfort. Try different positions but remember you cannot move from one spot. You can't walk around. You're stuck in line in one place.

Now try this. Make your feet too wide and stand still a minute or two in our imaginary line. What did you feel? What did you learn?

Now put your feet close together with your shoes touching. Stand like that for a minute or two. What did you feel? What did you learn?

Now, once again, stand for a minute or two and allow your body to tell you the most comfortable position of your feet.

75

You'll find if your feet are too far apart the large muscles of your lower body, your derriere and back will be in a strain. If your feet are too far apart you will quickly begin to feel uncomfortable. You couldn't wait for a bus in that position, could you? Why? Because the big muscles of your lower body are in a bind, in a strain and not working together. If your feet are too far apart your lower body is in a bio-mechanical bind. If your feet are too wide your muscles are fighting against one another and that's even before you swing at a golf ball.

You'll discover your feet and legs are in the most comfortable position when they are shoulder width.

Try this:

1. Imagine you're wearing pretty new white leather sneakers—an expensive gift from a friend.
2. Imagine a big five-gallon bucket full of red paint.
3. Stick both hands down into the red paint up to the wrists.
4. Stand up straight with your arms and hands hanging naturally at your side—with red paint dripping from your fingertips.
5. Make certain your feet are close enough together so the paint dripping off your fingers doesn't hit your new white shoes.
6. If your feet are too wide, you'll get red paint on your shoes.

That's how wide your feet should be to get the best out of your golf swing. That's how close together your feet should be to help your body to naturally twist and turn as you strike a golf ball. If your feet are shoulder width and no more your pretty white shoes won't ever be spotted with red paint, will they?

Quiet Feet

The Iron Byron

The golfer's feet must not be dancing, hopping, jumping, skipping, sliding, twisting or turning prior to impact.

The golfers must not hop, skip, jump, twist, slide or turn their feet prior to striking the golf ball.

The USGA has a golf machine to help them test golf balls and equipment. The machine is named the *Iron Byron* in honor of Mr. Byron Nelson. Mr. Nelson was a superb golfer. He finished in the top ten in sixty-five consecutive tournaments, won thirty-four times, finished second sixteen times and in 1945 he won eighteen times with eleven of those consecutive wins.

But golf wasn't Mr. Nelson's first love. Mr. Nelson loved ranching more than golf. When Mr. Nelson had won enough money to buy his ranch, build his house, build his barns, fence his property and purchase his cattle, he retired from golf at the age of 34. He spent the rest of his life in Texas with his lovely wife doing exactly what he loved to do. What might he have done if he had loved golf more than ranching?

Let's say someone gives us an Iron Byron golf machine. We're excited. We take it to the driving range to try it out. We set the Iron Byron on its table. We press the button and the golf machine hits the first ball perfectly. We put another ball in the golf machine and whack—another ball right down the middle. After a bucket of balls we see a puddle of balls in one spot in the distance. Our Iron Byron hit every ball perfectly. I wish I could do that.

The next day we invite some friends to observe our new golf machine in operation. We get our Iron Byron ready. After a couple of balls we hear a nasty snap. Oh dear. One of the legs on the golf machine's table has broken right in the middle. What shall we do?

I don't have replacement parts, but I do have a roll of Duck Tape. Yes, I know, but I say it that way and since I'm writing this book I'm going to spell it that way, too.

I don't want to disappoint my spectator friends so I make a jury-rigged splint for the broken table leg and wrap it as tightly as I can with duck tape. I load the hastily repaired golf machine with golf balls and press the button again. Whack.

Every time our golf machine begins its powerful downswing the table it's sitting on wiggles, shakes and wobbles because it has a crudely repaired broken leg. The poorly repaired table leg is not steady. Each time the golf machine swings, the golf ball goes a different direction because of the unpredictable movement of the supporting table. Oh dear. I have an unstable table. My once magnificent golf machine is no longer accurate. My friends watch in dismay as the perfectly good golf machine sprays golf balls all over the driving range like a duffer because of the unstable table.

It doesn't matter if it's Byron Nelson or me or you. If your table is unstable, you'll scatter your shots all over the golf course. In order to strike the golf ball consistently one must have a stable table.

Make certain your feet are firmly attached to the soil. Make certain the lower part of your golf machine is perfectly stable. Controlling your feet during your golf swing may take some work, but it will be worth it. If the golfer's lower body is moving, spinning, sliding, jumping, hopping—if the lower body is moving to a different place during each downswing, the top of the golf machine can never swing consistently. If the golfer's feet aren't quiet right up to the moment of impact, the golfer can never be a consistent ball striker.

Stabilize your lower body. Be in balance. Connect those shoes to the ground.

How do I know that? Every week one of the golf commentators will mention balance during the final round. Often they'll even show the feet of the balanced golfer during the swing.

The experts know there is no consistent ball striking without balance coming from the bottom half of the golfer's body.

Stabilize the bottom, then work on the top part.

Give up trying to use duck tape on your golf shoes. Keep those feet still. Just like Mr. Nelson and his machine, the successful golfer must have a stable table.

Weight Mostly on the Heels

The golfer's body is supported by the feet in the shoes, right? The golfer's shoes are the only thing touching the ground, right?

What is directly below the golfer's leg and ankle?

The heel of the golfer's foot is directly below the leg and ankle. Therefore, the weight of the golfer is supported by the leg, ankle and heel of the foot when the golfer is stationary.

The front part of the foot where the arch, ball and toes are located, gives added stability to the golfer's foot. The arch, ball and toes give humans the ability to walk, jump and run.

During the golf swing the golfer doesn't walk, jump or run. Therefore, the golfer's heel NEVER comes off the ground before impact.

Important: If the golfer's heels come off the ground prior to impact it makes the golfer taller and causes a change in the golfer's posture. If that change occurs during the downswing it causes inconsistent ball striking. In other words, if your feet are happy before impact you're likely to hit the ball over into someone's back yard rather than down the fairway or onto the green.

Knees Flexed

Proper golf posture must include flexed knees. The feeling should be that of squatting straight down by bending the knees—making the golfer shorter. The golfer MUST flex the knee joints.

The golfer's body collapses straight down like an accordion, but the head and chin stay up—which makes the spine rather straight. The straight spine makes it easy as pie for the golfer to rotate and smack that golf ball. In the address position the golfer MUST NOT bend over as if tying a shoelace. The head stays up and the spine fairly straight.

Try this: Stand up straight with your back against the wall. Then, with your back still firmly against the wall, bend your knees and make yourself about three or four inches shorter. You'll feel your straight back slide down the wall. The result is an excellent knee flex for the address position. Obviously, the golfer must tilt the spine to complete the address position but that's for a later chapter.

However, if instead bending your knees you bend over with a humped spine with your head down on your chest (a droopy cantaloupe), you can't rotate properly on the backswing.

Bend your knees. Squat down and bend your knees. Get your watermelon back out of the way of your golf swing as it passes your belt buckle and keep your cantaloupe UP.

Keep Your Watermelon Back

Push your watermelon backwards out of the way.

As you set your body to strike the golf ball, you must get your watermelon back out of the way to allow room for your hands to speed past your belt buckle as you strike the golf ball.

Imagine someone has given you a lovely tooled leather belt with a big yellow softball attached to the buckle. You love your softball belt and wear it to play golf. The big yellow softball on your new belt buckle sticks out in front of your tummy and gets in the way of your hands. Your golf pro friend, me of course, tells you not to worry. I like your softball belt. I got a softball belt for Christmas, too. I like to wear my softball belt when I play golf. I learned that all I have to do to strike the golf ball successfully is to get my softball back out of the way of my hands and I'll hit the golf ball fine. I have to move my watermelon backwards in order to move my softball out of the way to allow room for my hands at impact.

Take my advice and move your watermelon back, which then moves your softball back out of the way. You'll be amazed how well you strike the golf ball.

You'll find the golf ball easier to hit if at address you:

Bend your knees.
Get your watermelon and softball back out of the way.
Raise your cantaloupe up above your shoulder turn.

When you keep your cantaloupe up and your watermelon back the golfer's spine tends to straighten. When the golfer's spine is straight it rotates easily. If you have a good address position you'll discover, like magic, that the golf ball flies higher and longer towards the middle of the green.

How good is that?

The next time you go to the grocery store purchase a cantaloupe and a watermelon. Put them on the kitchen counter for a day or two. Every time you walk past think of this advice.

Back/Spine Straight

I know you think I'm repeating myself because I am repeating myself—intentionally.

Why do I repeat myself?

Don't you know the three laws of learning?

You don't know?

The first law of learning is repetition.

The second law of learning is repetition.

What is the third law of learning?

You guessed it—repetition.

Let's rehearse.
1. Grip the club and make sure the top thumb is covered.
2. Set the club behind the ball.
3. Set your body to the club.
4. Feet shoulder width—no more.
5. Bend the knees.
6. Watermelon back.
7. Cantaloupe up.
8. Align your body to the target line.

If your watermelon is back and your cantaloupe is up above the shoulder turn, then your back/spine will be moderately straight—and that's a good thing.

Do you know what a piano hinge is? If you take a piano hinge and kink it in the middle, will it hinge properly? Nope.

A careless golfer can't strike a golf ball with their cantaloupe drooping onto their chest which causes a curved spine. I can't tell you how many hundreds of times I've asked a student to put their watermelon back and get their cantaloupe up and the very next swing by the student was much better.

You can't get on the wrong bus and get to the right place.

Keep Your Cantaloupe Up

The golfer's cantaloupe must be UP. You must avoid a drooping cantaloupe at all costs.

The golfer's head, about the size of a cantaloupe, must be up above the golfer's shoulder turn during the swing. If the golfer's cantaloupe droops down onto the chest between the shoulders, it interferes with the shoulder turn and causes a multitude of problems. Keep your cantaloupe UP.

If you want to practice a little unethical gamesmanship and give the worst advice possible, you could kindly advise your opponent to keep their head down.

A drooping cantaloupe gets in the way of everything.

The golfer's shoulders rotate UNDER the golfer's chin. Therefore, the golfer's cantaloupe must be up. If the cantaloupe is droopy, the golfer's shoulder will rotate into the side of the cantaloupe. The golfer doesn't want their lead shoulder crashing into the side of their face on their backswing.

Keep your cantaloupe up during your golf swing.

Steady Head

A steady head is a must for consistent ball striking.

If you will combine a steady head with quiet feet the result will be consistent ball striking and you'll take home a few extra bucks after the round.

Add a proper grip to a steady head and quiet feet and you may end up a golf professional. You'll certainly be the best player on your block.

If your head and feet don't move during the swing, you don't have to worry about all the body parts in between getting lost. With a steady head and quiet feet the golfer can turn away from the target on the backswing and then swing down into the ball and be assured the club head will return to the ball with accuracy.

How does one keep a steady head? Here's a visual.

Imagine you're in the address position and the right side of your head and your right ear are tight up against a brick wall that cannot move. That would be the side of the golfer's head away from the target. In other words, the golfer's head CANNOT move to the right during the backswing.

Here's another thought that will help you have a steady head.

A few years ago I had the privilege to give a golf lesson to a gentleman 96 years of age. He was a retired businessman who worked all his professional life in Texas. In his younger days he was a member of the same golf club as Byron Nelson.

I have forgotten my student's name but I can still see him standing there before me taking his lesson. I remember he was polite and well spoken. He had a wonderfully smooth, rhythmic golf swing and a perfect grip.

My student said his ball striking was not what it should be. He couldn't figure out the problem. We worked on his swing. I remember we decided that he was having a balance issue and I encouraged him to squat a little lower in his address position which would give him a little more stability. It worked.

When the lesson was over my student mentioned he had played with Mr. Byron Nelson on quite a few occasions.

Byron Nelson was born near Waxahachi, Texas. I'm told the name Waxahachi came from an old language that means something like cow manure.

Mr. Nelson began caddying at Glen Garden Country Club near Fort Worth where he bested Ben Hogan in a 9 hole playoff for the caddy's championship. Mr. Nelson won 18 tournaments in 1945—11 in a row. He is considered by many the best ball striker the game of golf has ever known. When the PGA built a golf machine to help them determine the specs on golf clubs and golf balls, they called their precision machine the 'Iron Byron'. To tell the truth, according to the old guys who played with Mr. Nelson, they believe Mr. Nelson was actually a better ball striker than the machine.

As you can imagine, when my student said he had played golf with Byron Nelson, I was curious. I asked him if he had ever asked Mr. Nelson for golfing advice.

He said he did.

"What did you ask him? What did you ask him?" I eagerly asked.

I remember my excitement at that moment. I was actually talking to someone who had been given advice by Byron Nelson.

He said he asked Mr. Nelson what his most important swing thought was in his career. He said Mr. Nelson paused and looked him in the eye and grinned.

"You know, ever since I was a boy," Mr. Nelson said, "I've been looking down at the golf ball trying to see the face of the golf club as it makes contact with my golf ball. I'm always trying to see the golf club compress the ball at impact. I've been watching carefully to catch a glimpse of that moment since I was boy."

My student said Mr. Nelson paused once again, put another big grin on his face and looked my student straight in the eye.

"I've looked and looked. I watch every time I swing but I've never actually seen my golf club strike my golf ball in all these years. I guess the club-head is just traveling too fast for my eyes, but I keep watching my golf club hit my golf ball. I keep thinkin' that maybe one day, if I keep lookin', my eyes will catch up and I'll see the impact."

What lovely advice.

Mr. Nelson, my student and I give this wonderful advice to you freely today.

Watch the golf ball through impact. Keep a steady head with your eyes fixed on the ball you're about to hit. If you take Mr. Nelson's advice you might be pleasantly surprised when your golfing buddies start calling you a ball striking machine.

Both Arms Straight

Both arms should be straight at address. Both arms should be straight at address. Did I say both arms should be straight at address? If I forgot to say both arms are straight at address I guess I'll have to say it now, won't I?

When I tell you to have both arms straight I mean that the top part of your arm where the bicep is, and the bottom part of your arm where your forearm is should be in a line. The all the bones in your arm should be parallel.

If your arms are straight, about the only thing you should be able to get between your forearms when you're in the address position would be a tennis ball.

Your arms are way too far apart if you can get a soccer ball or a basketball between your arms at address.

As a beginner don't worry about your backswing too much. If you begin your swing with both arms straight you've begun very well indeed.

Both Arms Hang Straight Down

Both arms hang almost straight down from the shoulders.

Posture at address is critical. Remember, you can't get on the wrong bus and get to the right place.

If your watermelon is back and your cantaloupe is up, your spine will be tilted a bit towards the golf ball and your arms will hang almost straight down from your shoulder joints as you grasp the handle of the golf club.

Remember—the golf swing is up and down—not around.

Remember—the golf swing is a Ferris wheel—not a carousel.

A Ferris wheel goes up and down and back up again. A carousel goes around and around. The golf club doesn't go behind the golfer's back. The golf club goes UP.

Therefore, the golfer's arms hang straight down from the shoulder joints.

Beginning golfers always stand too far from the golf ball. Thus, their arms are extended out away from the body at more of a forty-five-degree angle to the ground rather than hanging straight down.

Because beginners stand too far from the golf ball they tend to top the ball frequently.

The golfer wants to stand close to the ball and take the head of the golf club pretty much directly away from the ball and up into the air—like a Ferris wheel. The head of the golf club doesn't go in a circle behind the back like a carousel. The golf club goes up and down.

When you address the golf ball, stand close enough to the ball so that your arms are hanging DOWN from the shoulder joints. Stand close to the golf ball and think FERRIS WHEEL.

Never ride a carousel and play golf. It won't work.

How to Align Correctly
The Big Paintbrush

Here is how to align your body correctly.

1. Stand behind the ball six or seven feet with the ball directly in a line between you and your target.
2. Imagine you are a professional painter.
3. Imagine you have a big bucket of florescent orange paint in one hand and a big wide paintbrush in the other. Your paintbrush is huge—about the size of a big thick telephone book. Remember those?
4. Using your imagination, paint a long straight line in florescent orange paint with your big wide brush all the way from your golf ball to your target.
5. As you stand six feet behind your golf ball, do you see that big wide orange florescent line running from your ball to the target?
6. Pick out something about five feet in front of your ball right in the middle of that wide florescent orange line to use as a marker when you address the ball. It might be a leaf, a twig, an old divot or a broken tee peg.
7. Now address the ball. (put your club head behind the ball, set your feet and body and get ready to hit the ball.)
8. As you address the ball, set your clubface squarely towards that leaf, twig or old divot you selected that was right in the middle of your imaginary orange line.

9. When you have the club head square to the marker you have selected you also have your club head square to your intended line of flight. Good for you.
10. Now give yourself and the club a pleasant tension-relieving waggle and you're ready to go. Because a golfer will naturally swing in a line parallel to their shoulder line, the golfer doesn't have to worry about where the ball will go if they have set up properly.

I've seen golfers put clubs down on the ground to check the alignment of their feet or hold the golf club in front of their waist or thighs to check the alignment of their lower body. The feet and thighs of the golfer do not determine alignment.

The golfer's arms are hooked onto the shoulders. Shoulder alignment is critical and the determining factor in where the ball will go.
The golfer should set the feet square to the intended line of flight and then match the should alignment.
Remember—the golfer's arms are attached to the shoulders—not the feet.
See that wide florescent line, pick out a near target five feet in front of the ball, set your clubface square to that near target you have chosen and then set your body to the club.

You're a good painter and you'll be a good golfer.
Hit it!

The Long Game

The Full Swing

Flyswatters, Hammers, Swingblades

If you want to learn how to hit a golf ball go get yourself a flyswatter and go around the house and swat imaginary flies.

Notice how you hold the flyswatter. Notice how you use your fingers, hand, wrist and arm.

You don't think much when you swat a fly, do you?

If you want to learn how to strike a golf ball go get yourself a claw hammer like we used to use in the olden days before the invention of nail guns.

Go find an old stump and get yourself a hat full of big nails and drive those big nails into the stump. Notice how you hold the hammer handle. Notice how you use your fingers, wrist, hand and arm.

You don't think much about swinging the hammer when you're driving a nail, do you? You do have to look at the nail head, don't you? What happens if you don't watch the nail head when you draw the hammer back and let it fall?

If you want to learn how to hit a golf ball straight and long go get yourself an old swingblade like I used to use to cut weeds. I bought a new one at 'Ace is the Place'. I guess if you don't want to buy a swingblade you can use your 9 iron instead.

I keep my swingblade in my truck to help my students get a feel for the golf swing. Harvey Penick agrees with me. He said the old swingblade is the best training aid ever made for the golf swing. Most of the gimmicky things advertised on the TV today are pretty much useless.

Get yourself a swingblade and spend a few hours lopping off dandelion heads—as Harvey Penick says and you'll do yourself a big favor.

You don't think much about your swing when your daddy makes you spend half a day cutting the weeds in the field out by the barn. When you use your manual swingblade weed cutter notice how you hold it. Notice how effortlessly you swing—mostly because you wish you were doing something else.

Harvey Pinick says the old swing blade weed cutter is the best swing training aid you can buy.

And on your way home from the hardware store, go by the bookshop and buy Harvey Penick's *Little Red Book*. He knows a lot more about teaching golf than I ever will.

One Effortless Swing for All Clubs

One swing

One swing speed

One grip

One stance

One posture

One smooth, consistent tempo

A golfer should swing with the same smooth swing no matter which club they're using. The golfer has fourteen clubs in the bag and only one swing.

The golfer doesn't swing harder to make the ball go farther. Whether you're using your driver or your nine iron you want to use the same consistent swing for both clubs. You should use the same swing for short clubs and the long clubs—one swing for all clubs.

Let the club do the work.

Let the club hit the ball farther.

It isn't true that the faster you take the club away from the ball the faster you can swing down at the ball. I know that sounds kinda stupid, but a lot of folks fall into that trap. The golfer should develop a smooth consistent tempo as they take the club away, make the transition move at the top and swing down and through impact—all in one effortless motion.

Never be a herky-jerky golfer. Have one smooth tempo when you take a full swing with any club in your bag. Aren't you glad you don't have one club and fourteen swing?

Be a smooth swinger. Don't be a jerk.

The Golf Swing – Smooth as Silk

Don't be a jerk.

A smart golfer will develop one smooth swing for his fourteen clubs—not fourteen swings.

The transition from the backswing to the downswing is the most important part of your golf swing. The transition is the point at which things often go wrong.

The biggest enemy of a successful golf swing is a short, quick backswing that begins its downward path to the golf ball with a jerk.

Be smooth. Finish your backswing with leisure.

It doesn't matter how fast you take your backswing, there comes a point when the club must stop going away from the ball, reverse its course, and begin its downward path towards impact. This transition is the most important part of your golf swing. Make it smooth as silk. No need to rush this most important moment.

Make this transition smooth and your chances of a good impact with the ball are greatly improved!

Snatch the club away from the ball—take a quick, jerky, out of control swing and you'll look like the Tasmanian Devil and you'll play like the Tasmanian Devil.

A smooth effortless transition into your downswing with quiet feet will give the golfer better control of the golf club and give the best chance of a repeatable and consistent golf swing.

A wise golfer will develop the idea that the golf ball gets in the way of a smooth, effortless swing.

Golf isn't rocket science. It's not complicated. Work on the simple, straight forward fundamentals and you'll strike the ball better. Develop one smooth consistent swing for all the clubs. Develop one swing and one speed for all clubs.

There is no elusive secret to better ball striking. That new set of golf clubs you see advertised during the golf tournament won't magically lower your score. You're not going to read a golf magazine and discover the single tip that will change your game.

Never try to hit the ball. Always try to swing through the ball with a smooth rhythm.

Wind up and then unwind in one smooth controlled motion.

The golfer has the same swing for a shot of a hundred yards as for a shot of a hundred and fifty yards. The golfer doesn't swing harder or faster to make the ball go farther. The golfer swings the six iron the same as the nine iron. The ball goes farther with the six iron because the six iron has a lower loft. It won't go farther because you hit it harder.

The loft of the club head and the length of the shaft determine the distance the golf ball will travel when struck. Develop one controlled swing and choose a different club for a different distance. Never adjust your swing speed.

The biggest enemy of a smooth golf swing is a short quick backswing that begins its downward path to the golf ball prematurely with a jerk. FINISH YOUR BACKSWING.

The transition from the backswing to the downswing is the most important part of your golf swing. It's at this transition point where most of our golf swing inconsistencies originate.

It doesn't matter how fast you take your backswing, there comes a point when the club must stop going away from the ball, reverse its course, and begin its path down and towards the golf ball and impact. This transition is the most important part of your golf swing. Make it smooth as silk. No need to rush this most important moment. The club must change direction at transition. No hurry to get there.

Make this transition smooth and your chances of a good impact with the ball are greatly improved.

Snatch the club away from the ball, take a jerky, out of control swing, and you'll look and play like the Tasmanian Devil.

A smooth effortless transition into your downswing with quiet feet will give the golfer better control of the golf club and give you the best chance of a repeatable and consistent golf swing and crisp ball striking. Squeeze the trigger. Don't snatch at it.

Don't Be A Jerk.

Ball Position is Critical

One swing and 3 ball positions.

The short, lofted clubs must swing down at the golf ball and take a divot of earth after you strike the golf ball.

As the clubs get longer and have less loft, the bottom of the club head doesn't go as deep into the soil.

The fairway woods just brush the soil. The driver, the longest club of all and the one with the least loft, doesn't touch the soil at all.

All the short-shafted clubs should be played about five inches from the left heel. Practically, this turns out to be in the middle of the stance.

The long irons and hybrids should be played slightly closer to the front foot—about 3 inches from the left heel.

All of the woods, the driver, 3 wood, 5 wood, 7 wood, should be played just off the left heel.

Therefore, I teach 3 ball positions.

1. In the middle of the stance for lofted clubs.
2. 3 inches from the left heel for long irons and hybrids.
3. Just off the left heel for the fairway woods and driver.

The Swing is a Ferris Wheel

Swing up and down like a Ferris wheel.
Not around, like a carousel.

The head of the golf club goes back directly away from the ball—then up into the air and then back down and through the ball—and up into the air on the follow through.

The golf club doesn't go around in a circle behind the golfer's back.

The golf swing is more like a Ferris wheel than a carousel.

One-Piece Take Away

The arms, hands and club should move away from the ball at least twelve inches with NO BREAKING OF THE WRISTS.

The shoulders move but the wrists do not begin to cock whatsoever in the first move away from the ball. During the first twelve inches the club head travels away from the ball on the backswing, the wrists should NOT cock in the least. The shoulders, arms, wrists and club should move as one. Thus, it's called a one-piece takeaway.

Here's a way to feel that:

1. Take your driver.
2. Hold the driver so far down the shaft the handle of the club is tight against your torso.
3. Keep your arms straight.
4. Hold the club head six inches off the ground or floor.
5. Move the club head left and right, farther and farther, keeping the butt end of the driver tight against your torso and not moving and keeping your arms straight.
6. You find when you move the club head left and right and keep the handle snug against your body you'll find you can't use your wrists whatsoever.
7. The triangle formed by your two arms and your shoulders is the only thing moving left and right.
8. This is the feeling you should have for the first 12 inches of your backswing. It's called a one-piece takeaway. No wrist cock in the first 12 inches of the backswing.

Steady Head – Quiet Feet

The golfer should have a steady head during the swing. If the golfer's head stays in one place, and if the golfer's feet don't move during the swing, the golfer can return the club head back to the ball with consistency.

If the golfer's head doesn't sway left and right or bob up and down and if the golfer's feet stay where they're supposed to, all the stuff in the middle between the head and feet can twist and turn and the club head will go right back where it's supposed to.

If your head stays in one place when you swing and if your feet stay at home when you swing then don't worry about all the things in between. All those body parts in middle can't get lost and you'll hit the ball with consistency.

First - Waist High to Waist High

This is the beating heart of the golf swing.

Here's how to learn to make a full swing at the golf ball. When you're learning to swing or when you want to put the wheels back on, here's a little drill that I've found quite useful.

1. Address the ball on a low tee-peg with an eight iron.
2. Pick out a precise target line. Distance isn't critical with this drill.
3. Feet should be shoulder width and no more.
4. Ball placed in the middle of the stance.
5. Arms straight. (elbows not bent)
6. In the address position, the handle of the club should be pointing at your belly button—not your hip joint. (if your belly button isn't in the middle then point the handle of the club in the middle of your tummy)
7. Except for having one hand lower than the other on the handle of the golf club, everything else is symmetrical, isn't it?
8. Weight evenly distributed and more towards the heels than the toes.
9. Knees flexed, hips flexed, watermelon back and cantaloupe up. (this straightens your spine)
10. Swing waist high to waist high with very little wrist break. Don't swing the club head past waist high.
11. When you swing, let the club do the work. The ball won't go too far but that's ok. You're getting a FEEL for the heart of the golf swing.

12. During the swing the shoes and feet don't move—not at all—none, nada, zilch, zip.
13. The hips and knees move very little. You want to have a stable table.
14. Swing through the golf ball—never slap at the golf ball. The golf ball gets in the way of a smooth, rhythmic swing. Don't be a jerk.
15. Finish waist high on the follow-through—no more.
16. Remember to use very little wrist break.

This is the heart of the golf swing. You'll be surprised how easy it is to hit the golf ball substantial distances with a waist high to waist high swing. Anytime the wheels fall off, go back to this drill. You might even end up playing with this swing. When you can hit a whole bucket of balls with consistency with this swing then you might add a little shoulder turn and some more wrist cock on the backswing but be careful. If you put too much salt in the stew it won't be fit to eat, will it? A little of most things goes a long way.

This is the heart of the golf swing. You'll be surprised how easy it is to hit the golf ball substantial distances with a waist high to waist high swing. Remember—don't move those shoes.

Extension – Stretch and Stretch

Ok. You're ready to swing. You know how to set up. You understand you must have quiet feet. You understand perfectly about a one piece take-away. You have hit several buckets of balls with a waist high to waist high swing. What do you do now?

I love the idea of a waist high to waist high effortless swing.

Add this to your effortless swing:

1. On your backswing stretch your left arm away from your body.
2. Then swing through the golf ball with both arms straight.
3. Then, after impact, stretch your right arm down the target line just as if you're pointing where you want the ball to go.

When you begin your swing take the club away from the ball and stretch out your left arm (if you're right handed).

After you make contact, stretch your right arm straight towards the target.

Stretching your left on your backswing and stretching your right on your follow-through will give you full extension and make your striking of the golf ball much more consistent.

Take the club away—stretch the left arm.

Swing through the ball.

Then stretch the right arm down the target line.

After Waist High, the Umbrella

After you have become comfortable with the waist high to waist high swing you can increase the length of the backswing.

Instead of stopping the backswing at the waist high position you can continue the backswing to the umbrella position.

What is the umbrella position? On the backswing the golfer's club passes waist high, the golfer's wrist will cock and the shaft of the club will point at the sky—as if the golfer were holding an umbrella out to the side.

On the backswing in the umbrella position the golfer holds the club as far away from the left shoulder as possible and the wrists cock which holds the shaft of the golf club vertical—in the umbrella position.

The opposite is true of the follow through. The right arm extends towards the target and the wrists cock holding the club head vertical on the follow through. This should be an easy, effortless motion.

Let the Club do the Work

If you want to be frustrated, if you want to spray the golf ball all over the golf course, if you want to be disheartened and wonder why it is you can't seem to improve your ball striking, then swing fast, quick and hard. If you never want to improve, swing has hard and fast as you can. If you want to be a terrible golfer, use all your strength when you swing. That's a sure way to be the worst player in your foursome.

If you want to be a good ball striker, hit accurate shots towards your target and get better and better every year, then swing with an effortless ease. Let the club do the work.

I was a member of my high school golf team. Being on the golf team was one of the greatest joys of my life. I can't tell you how much fun that was. It was our four guys competing against their four guys. Each of us played an eighteen hole match against one of their players.

I remember one match vividly. From the very first hole I didn't do well. After about 6 or 7 terrible holes I was way behind my opponent. I hadn't won a hole. I was disgusted as only a teenage boy can be disgusted. My world was in darkness.

What did I do? I gave up, of course. I decided I was done. Foolishly I quit. I didn't actually walk off the golf course but from that moment I didn't care where the ball went. I knew I was going to lose so I quit trying. When it was my turn to play I remember walking up to the ball and hitting it without any thought or preparation.

The unexpected happened. I began playing well—very well. I couldn't believe it. After I gave up I must have relaxed and swung the golf club like I had practiced. I didn't win the match but I've never forgotten that instructive afternoon.

If you want to be a good ball striker learn to relax and swing with effortless ease. Let the club and gravity combine to hit the golf ball. You don't hit a golf ball with brute force and ignorance. Unwanted muscular tension is the number one enemy of a good golf swing. If you want to experience how I felt as a disgusted, disappointed teenager, then swing as hard and fast as you can using brute force and ignorance.

Feet Flat at Impact

Keep your feet flat on the ground through impact. Well, if you don't believe me, look at some pictures (not Bubba Watson).

My advice is purchase several of the very best golf magazines. Get yourself a scrapbook. Cut out all the pictures of professional men and woman at all stages of the golf swing. Study the pictures. Emulate what you see.

Don't read anything or take any written advice in the golf magazines. Most of what is written is for low handicap or scratch golfers. Those guys who write those articles are trying their best to come up with something new. There is nothing new in the golf swing—not one thing.

Can you imagine standing on a sheet of solid ice and trying to hit a golf ball while you are wearing slick, leather-soled shoes? Good luck.

Well, if you move your feet before impact that's just about what you're trying to do—hit a golf ball while moving.

Keep your feet perfectly still until AFTER impact.

Finish in Balance

Learn how to put the car in the garage.

After impact the golfer should finish in balance. The golfer's foot closest to the target should still be exactly where it was at address (left for righties and right for lefties). The lead foot NEVER moves.

I heard Gary Player describe the finish as taking the golf club up the hill and putting it in the garage. He described the top end of the golf club as the tail lights of the car. After impact, the golf club continues to travel up the hill until it's parallel with the ground with the top of the handle of the golf club pointing at the target—just as if it was in the garage with the tail lights looking at the flag. I love it.

You'll often see professional golfers taking a swing and holding their pose after their finish. They don't do that to look good for the camera. Young golfers are taught to 'hold the pose' for a few moments to make certain that they were in perfect balance after the golf swing.

It's impossible to hit a golf ball if you're stumbling. It's impossible to hit a golf ball with consistency if you're out of balance at the moment of impact. Stay in balance. Learn to put the car in the garage with one smooth motion. Keep your lead foot stationary before, during and after the swing and be in perfect balance when you put the car in the garage and you'll be a good golfer indeed and you'll make Gary Player proud.

Glossary of Golfing Terms

Address Position - The physical position of the golfer's body when ready to strike the golf ball.

Away - A golfer is said to be away when the golfer's ball is farthest from the hole of any player in the group. If a golfer is away, it is that golfer's turn to play. The person who is the greatest distance from the hole always plays first.

Backswing - The first part of the golf swing. The backswing begins when the golfer takes the head of the golf club away from its address position directly behind the golf ball. On the backswing the golfer takes the club away from the ball and away from the target. The backswing continues until the golfer stops the club, reverses the club head's path and begins the downswing and impact with the golf ball.

Backwards – A word to describe most everything the golfer does when trying to strike a golf ball. Golf is like looking in a mirror when you're backing a trailer—everything is the opposite of what you would think. If you want the ball to go to the right, you swing to the left. If you want the ball to go up, you swing down. If you want to hit the ball a long way you relax and swing easy. Oh well.

Ballmark – A ballmark is the depression left on the green by the impact of a descending golf ball. It is good etiquette to repair all ballmarks your ball makes in the surface of the putting green.

Unrepaired ballmarks make for bumpy putting. Experienced golfers always help care for the golf course.

Birdie - A score on a hole of 1 under par. I hope you have a lot of them.

Bladed Shot - A shot struck exactly on the equator of the golf ball by the bottom lower edge of an iron. The resulting ball flight is low to the ground and unpredictable—and ugly.

Bogey – One over par. An ok score but not great.

Bouncing – What basketball players do with the basketball. Not recommend for the golfer's lower body during the golf swing.

Caddy – A person who carries the golf bag for a player. All golfers are allowed to have a caddy by the rules of golf. A caddy is the only person allowed to give a golfer advice during play.

Chicken Wing - Premature bending of the lead elbow at impact—the left arm for righties and the right arm for lefties.

Chip Shot - This is a low trajectory shot that intentionally stays about knee high and mostly rolls to its target. A chip shot spends more time on the ground rolling than in the air. This shot is often made with a 6 or 7 iron.

Closed Face - A term which describes the clubface at address turned to hit the ball to the left side of the target line for a right-handed golfer.

Cut Shot – A shot intentionally played to bend to the right for a right-handed golfer.

Dancing – Something a boy and a girl do on a dance floor on Friday and Saturday night. Not recommended during a golf swing.

Divot - The depression in the soil left behind when the bottom of a golf club takes away the soil at the moment of striking the golf ball. The golf club must hit the ground at the bottom of the arc of the golf swing. The club strikes the ball and the soil at exactly the same moment. The divot, the removal of the soil, occurs after impact with the golf ball. Golfers should replace their divots and fill divots with sand.

Downswing - The part of the swing after the transition that begins the club's downward path to strike the golf ball.

Double Bogey – A score of two over par on a given hole. Learn not to have too many double bogies.

Draw - A shot that moves slightly from right to left for a right-handed golfer.

Driver - The name of the club that hits the ball the longest distance. It has the lowest loft of any club in the bag—sometimes called the "1-Wood".

Eagle - A score of two under par on a golf hole. I hope you see many of these rare birds.

Explosion Shot - This term refers to a shot from a bunker or sand trap that takes a large quantity of sand with the ball and gives the appearance of an explosion of sand and/or soil.

Extension – This term refers to the full extension of the arms during the golf swing. A straight and extended left arm on the backswing, both arms straight at impact and a straight right arm on the follow through. Full extension at these three points gives the golfer the biggest swing arc possible, the best chance of consistency and will permit the greatest clubhead speed.

Fade - A term that describes a ball flight that bends slightly to the right for a right-handed golfer.

Fairway – The closely mown area between the tee box and the green. In the fairway golf shots are the easiest because the grass is short and doesn't get between the club head and the ball at impact.

Fairway Wood - A wood used to hit the ball longer distances when in the fairway—not on the tee box. The club head is designed to hit the ball lying on the grass of the fairway. Many players will carry a 3 wood and a 5 wood.

Fairway Metal - A modern word sometimes used for fairway woods. The word is used by sports commentators in an attempt to change the nomenclature of the game. I've noticed they still call a pitching wedge a pitching wedge even though it hasn't been used for pitching since the invention of the sand wedge.

Finish - This is the part of the swing after striking the golf ball. It is also called the follow-through. It has nothing to do with Finland.

Follow-through - This is the part of the swing after striking the golf ball. It is also called the finish.

Gagger - A long putt that unexpectedly falls into the hole and makes the putter's opponents 'gag' in disbelief.

Gimme – A ball that is so close to the hole an opponent will give you the putt without asking you to putt out.

Grain – The term used to describe the way grass grows on the ground, especially on the putting green. Grass doesn't grow straight up. Grass tends to grow towards the setting sun. Grain can very much affect the roll of the ball on a green. The golf ball will tend to follow the grain—therefore the grain of the grass on the green can alter the path of the golf ball.

Green - The closely mown area of the golf course where the hole is placed. The greens are cut short and smooth each day to provide the golf ball a predictably even surface when the golfer is putting.

Grip - The manner in which a golfer holds the golf club.

Grooves - The grooves in the face of the golf club help the club grip the ball and give the golf ball spin when struck.

Grounding the Club - Placing the club head behind the ball and touching the ground with the bottom of the club head. Grounding the club is not permitted in hazards. Hazards are marked by red or yellow stakes. Sand traps are considered hazards although they will not have stakes around them.

Handle - The part of the club the hands hold. Also called the grip.

Hazards - The part of the golf course marked by yellow or red stakes. The rules are different for hazards. For example: the golfer can't ground the club head in a hazard. A hazard is a place where you don't want to be.

Heel of the Club - The part of the club head nearest to where the shaft attaches to the club head. The end of the clubface away from the heel is the toe.

Hopping – Something rabbits do with their feet when they're heading down the bunny trail. Generally not recommend during the golf swing.

Hook - A term that describes a ball's flight that curves strongly to the left for right-handed golfers.

Hosel - The rounded part of the heel of an iron golf club which attaches the shaft to the head. It is also called the shank. I don't have to tell you that you don't want to hit the ball with the shank of your golf club. You won't like the result.

Hybrid - Golf clubs that have a combination of features of both irons and woods. Hybrid clubs are more forgiving than the old-style irons.

Impact - The moment at which the club strikes the ball in the golf swing.

Irons – The term applies to clubs made of solid metal. In the olden days it was a term that applied to the clubs that used to be made of iron or steel instead of wood. In the olden days the long clubs would have a wooden head and the shorter clubs, the irons, would be made of solid metal. Today, the term applies to the clubs that are not hybrids, woods or wedges.

Jumping - Something athletes do in a great many sports. Something frogs do. Not recommended during a golf swing.

Kangaroo – An animal in Australia who hops everywhere he goes. Plays poor golf. Can't keep his feet still.

Lag Putt - A lag putt is a putt from a long distance away from the hole. A golfer is happy to stop the ball close to the hole when lag putting.

Lob Wedge - A 60-degree wedge. It is used around the green for pitching because it hits the ball higher than a 56° sand wedge and a lot higher than a 45° pitching wedge.

Loft - Loft is the measurement of the angle of the clubface which determines how high or low a club hits the ball into the air. Loft determines the golf ball's launch angle. For the wedges and the irons the golfer will have about 4° difference in loft between clubs. With the woods and long hybrids there is often about 3° difference in loft. Loft in this case has nothing to do with the upper part of a barn.

Metals – The modern word often used by annoying golf commentators to describe the long clubs that hit the ball the longest distances. The word 'metal' replaces the old word 'wood'. In the olden days the heads of the long clubs were made of a hard, dense wood like persimmon. Today, the long clubs are made of metal. I still call my pitching wedge a pitching wedge and not a 10 iron and I call my long clubs woods—so there.

Mulligan – Not in the rules of golf but should be. A mulligan is given when a golfer is allowed to hit a second ball in place of their first.

One-Piece Takeaway - One-piece takeaway is the term used to describe the first 10 inches or so of the backswing when everything moves as one piece. The shoulders, arms and torso move as one. There should be no wrist movement at all in the first few inches. None of the body parts move independently during the one-piece takeaway.

Open Stance - The position of the body at address in which the body is open towards the target. For a right-handed person the left shoulder is moved to the left which turns the body so that the golfer's chest is slightly facing the target. Usually this means pulling the left foot back a little from the target line. An open stance is used if a golfer wants to bend the ball to the right—for a right-handed golfer.

Other – A very high score on a golf hole—so high the golf commentators don't bother to give it a name.

Out-of-Bounds - This is the border of the golf course where the players are allowed to play. Out-of-bounds is usually marked by a series of white stakes but sometimes by a wall, fence or road. Out-of-bounds will usually be listed on the score card if unusual. Players should never go across the out-of-bounds markers to retrieve a golf ball.

Par - A regulation score on a golf hole.

Part Shot – Any shot that is executed with less than a full swing. When a golfer nears the green, the golfer will reach a point at which any shot with any club the golfer chooses will be executed with only a partial swing—not a full swing.

Pin - A term used for the flagstick on the green.

Pitch Shot - A high trajectory shot that spends more time in the air than on the ground. It usually stops quickly. The most common club used for pitching is the sand wedge.

Pitching Wedge - The next higher lofted club in a set after the 9 iron. There is usually 4 degrees loft between irons. The word pitching wedge is an old term given when the pitching wedge was the highest lofted club in the golfer's bag. The pitching wedge today is usually about 45° and should not be used today for pitching.

Posture - The term that describes how a golfer stands to prepare to strike the golf ball—the position of the golfer's body at address.

Pre-shot Routine - This is a set routine experienced golfers use before every shot to insure they remember important aspects of ball striking. They will have different routines for different shots and different clubs. A pre-shot routine also prevents experienced golfers from unwanted thoughts just prior to striking the golf ball. Did I let the cat out? Did I forget to turn off the stove?

Pull Shot – A shot hit straight to the left of the target. A pull doesn't bend like a hook.

Range Finder – A device used to measure exact distances on the golf course. According to the rules, it is legal to use a range finder in competitive golf. It is critical to know the exact distance from your ball to the pin or to your intended landing area. Since the flagstick is moved to a different location every day, a laser range finder will tell you the exact distance to the flag. Unless you're using a professional caddy, knowing the exact distance to the flag by using a laser range finder is essential for accuracy.

Regulation - A term used to describe the number of shots an expert golfer would take to play a given hole. A par-3 hole should be played in three shots, a par-4 hole should be played in four shots.

Sand Wedge - The club most frequently used for getting out of a sand trap or for a pitch shot into the green. A sand wedge is usually 56° degrees. It was invented by Gene Sarazen in 1932.

Scooping - What you do when you get ice cream out of the carton. Something done with a ladle, dipper, bucket or shovel. Not something one does with a golf club in the short game.

Shaft - The part of the club that connects the head of the golf club to the handle.

Shank - The part of the shaft that connects the head of the golf club to the shaft. Shank is also a term for a shot that is struck with an iron where the clubhead joins the shaft—thus the ball hits the clubhead on the shank. When the ball strikes the rounded part of the heel of the iron it causes the ball to glance off the face at a sharp angle to the right of the intended line of flight for a right-handed golfer.

A shank is the ugliest, most hateful shot in golf. If you don't believe me, ask any experienced golfer. It is good etiquette to never think that word, much less say it out loud. Sam Snead would never give a golf lesson to a person who shanked the ball.

Short Game - That part of the golf game that requires less than a full swing—usually around 70 yards from the green and closer. The short game uses partial swings many call 'part shots'.

Short Irons – The most lofted irons—the irons that the golfer uses when closer to the green. Usually considered the 7, 8, 9, and pitching wedge.

Skating – Skating is sliding around on ice. It's something figure skaters do in the Olympics and Canadians do when they play hockey. Not recommended when you swing at a golf ball.

Skipping – Something carefree children do when they feel especially good. Not recommended during the golf swing.

Skull Shot - A ball that is struck exactly on the equator by the bottom leading edge of an iron. The resulting ball flight travels just above the ground and is unpredictable—and very ugly. A skulled shot usually goes over the green, down the hill and winds up in the pond.

Stable Table – A term referring to the stability of a golfer's lower body, especially the feet. During the golf swing the golfer's feet should not hop, jump, slide or twist.

Sliding – Something kids do in the snow. Not recommended for a golfer's feet during the golf swing.

Swaying – Something trees do in a strong wind. Something dancers do on the dance floor. Even a small amount of sway is not recommended during the golf swing.

Swing Blade - Sometimes called a sling blade. It is a weed cutting tool from last century used before the invention of the mechanical weed wacker. Recommended by Harvey Pinick, and I concur, as the best swing training tool available to learn how to swing at a golf ball.

Swing Thought – A single idea that a golfer has in the mind at some point before or during the golf swing.

Tap-in – A very short putt that is so close to the hole you couldn't miss it.

Target Line - An imaginary line that runs through the golf ball directly towards the target.

Toe of the club - The part of the club head farthest from where the shaft joins the club head.

Top Shot - A term for a shot that strikes only the very top of the golf ball. A ball that has been topped rolls on the ground after being struck—not a pretty sight. Topped shots are usually caused by golfers standing too far from the golf ball.

Transition - The point at the end of the backswing where the club stops going backward and begins the downswing towards the golf ball and impact.

Triangle - Used to describe the shape of the arms and shoulders at the address position. Holding the triangle in the first part of the backswing is essential in a one-piece takeaway.

Up and Down - A term referring to the player's ability to get the ball up on the green and down into the hole in only two shots from relatively close range. A good short game player will be able to get "up and down" quite often.

Waltz – Very romantic under the moonlight with your sweetie but terrible to try while you're trying to hit a golf ball.

Waggle – An important tension relieving movement of the club head by the hands immediately prior to taking the backswing.

Woods – The old and proper name for the long clubs. In the olden days the heads of the long clubs were made of wood— often a very hard wood like persimmon. The modern driver, 3-wood, 5-wood etc. are made entirely of metal. I still call them woods. I can't seem to manage to say 'fairway metal'. It just doesn't sound right. I still call the pitching wedge the pitching wedge. I can't seem to call it the 10 iron.

A Golf Poem

I am one of the most fortunate people in all the world to have played a game I love all my life and to have the honor of sharing what I know with others.

One of my students wrote this little poem for me after a particularly successful lesson. A friend of mine said that some folks might think me a bit arrogant to include this in my book— especially with the line that says I'm the best, but everyone knows to take that with a grain of salt. I thought this a sweet effort and I was touched. Perhaps at that one particular moment, I was the best.

I promise not to think ill of you if you publish a little book and put a poem in there about yourself.

Barney's Golf Poem

The game of golf is a challenge for me.
I sometimes hit the ball by a nearby tree.
I needed someone who could really help me.
So I turned to the best, and his name is Bar-ney.

I pitched and hit and drove the ball.
I sometimes lost my balance and would almost fall.
He taught me to keep my feet still.
And loft the ball over the hill.

My arms now hold straight.
My posture is great.
I'm even trying to use club number eight.

I have to thank him for he is the best.
And now I can play as good as the rest.

Notes

Notes

Notes

Notes

Notes

Notes

Notes

Notes

Notes

28 November 2021

Printed in Great Britain
by Amazon

f229b459-1088-47a9-a184-502ffa77baf6R01